GOD DOESN'T CARE WHAT YOU WEAR™

THE LIMITATIONS OF OUR BELIEFS

BY BEVERLY LUTZ

 **FriesenPress**

Suite 300 - 990 Fort St
Victoria, BC, Canada, V8V 3K2
www.friesenpress.com

ISBN
978-1-4602-5982-5 (Hardcover)
978-1-4602-5983-2 (Paperback)
978-1-4602-5984-9 (eBook)

1. Body, Mind & Spirit

Distributed to the trade by The Ingram Book Company

CONTENTS

"The author shares her fascinating life experiences with clarity, personal truth and translucency. In reading, we access our own reality, being gently persuaded to peel away the distorting layers of an inauthentic existence in order to achieve a life of harmony coming from our own personal truths. Beverly's journey is one we all need to take."

Joanne Ford, designer, entrepreneur.

"Beverly cuts through our illusions with precision, insight and freshness to uncover the truth that has always been shining through to our lives. This book shares we are in perfect form, regardless of our histories and life stories. Nothing needs to change except our illusions and beliefs."

Denise McTighe, writer, artist.

"Beverly's provocative insights provide a framework for examining the binding chains of illusory beliefs, freeing our hearts for joyful participation in our own life's journey. As with all the great teachers, her example and call for self honest reflection is equally an acknowledgement and an eye with which to view the perfect imperfections of All That Is in comprising the mosaic of the divine beauty of life."

Majella O'Gaillín, Student/Client.

CHAPTER ONE:

Just Begin

We must be willing to get rid of the life we've planned, so as to have the life that is waiting for us.

Joseph Campbell

This tale of insights, grace, and astonishment has been an exceedingly vulnerable thing for me to do, unlike anything I have ever done before. By virtue of the fact that you are reading this, I have released these writings into the ethers. I have no defense against my own act, because I now cannot take these words back. I have written an exposé of my life and I feel exposed. I wrote a poem years back, the first part of which poignantly describes how I feel in writing these opening lines:

> *Cut open wide*
>
> *like a salmon,*
>
> *the red raw vibrating flesh*

splayed, pinned to the earth

while eagle plucks

vision from her wounds

to feed the food of growth

into its namesake.

Writing this book has also been an affirmation of my inner knowing that life truly unfolds in spite of me. And with that knowing has come an enormous freedom. So even though I feel vulnerable, I also trust the forces that set me at my computer and wrote these words that came pouring out of my fingers.

In this book I use the stories of my life to lead you, the reader, into a provocative, introspective space. The stories tell of certain significant people and experiences along my journey. How these people came into my life and how my life events unfolded with them are—for me—sheer magic, leaving me ever astonished. It is through such encounters, such stories, that I have gained insight and learned to dig deeper within myself.

Although the stories serve to illustrate life's unfoldings, they are nevertheless only stories. And within the field of the collective consciousness, there is no tale that has been left untold. For example, a lack of self-worth or a tragic death has been played out many times, in many ways. What is important and unique *to you* lies in the underbelly of the story, the place where gems are waiting to be discovered. My characters will be different from yours, my buttons that get pushed by events will be different from yours, and yet in my experiences the opportunity for insight is there for you, too. Notice which pieces of my stories land on you—stir your inner pot, as I like to say—and perhaps point you in the direction of unfinished business in your life.

No names are used in this journal of my life. Although some of you may be able to identify yourselves and thus perhaps others, my intent is to keep everyone unidentifiable to the general reader. None of the stories are about the person per se, rather they are used to illustrate a point from which I gained insight.

Although my own family has been and is most significant in my life, out of respect for the privacy of my children and theirs, I have not spoken about any events personally concerning them.

I have felt compelled to write, for myself, as part of my journey before it is over. It has been a difficult process, at times; I have felt raw and utterly exposed in my public vulnerability. Yet, at the same time, I remain astonished at the perfection of the unfolding, of the magic, of the *mystery* that is all *life*.

I often see, in working with people, how the magic is lost on them through the "don't likes," "why me?" and "don't wanna' haves" in their lives. Perhaps through my sharing you will experience a shift in your perception and see the perfection of your own journey, without the need to change any of it. If this happens, my vulnerability will have been of service. Experiencing life as it is without the desire to change it is not to say you have acquiesced or given up— on the contrary. In simply releasing resistance to life as it is, there comes a shift in perspective that opens us into exhilarating freedom.

Although I wasn't initially aware that my writing would turn into the personal story that it has, it became clear after a long conversation with a close friend that it would take this form. As we discussed our lives in intimate detail, we came to a depth of realization—more profound than ever before—of how each event in our lives has led us magically into the next. The interconnection of the unfolding is often only visible when we look back. When we do, we see also how our lives truly do unfold in spite of us.

I wrote this book not simply as storytelling (much as I enjoy that) but rather as inspiration for you to look back on your life and learn for yourself how your life has unfolded, with Grace present at all times and with little actual participation from you.

I kept asking the question: "Where do I begin?" And the answer always came back: "Just begin."

"What day is today?" asked Pooh.

"It's today," squeaked Piglet.

"My favorite day!" said Pooh.

A. A. Milne, Winnie-the-Pooh

CHAPTER TWO:
Expiration Date

Live today as though it is your last, and one day it will be.

Anonymous

For me, the above quotation is like a mantra, serving to remind me of my own mortality. I repeat it often, to myself and to others, in my own attempt to stay aware. In the literal reality of this physical life, I could be dead tomorrow. Although we may all be aware of such simple, profound statements about life, we tend not to live our lives accordingly. For example, what is true for me, true for you, and true for everyone living in a physical body is that there will come a time when our own unique expiration date will have been reached, and we will die. We will be no more—*we will cease to exist.* Will our clock stop ticking in the next five minutes? Or tomorrow? Will the end come with a bang or a whimper? Or will it be a drawn-out protest that ends in inevitable acceptance and surrender? Beyond a doubt, we know that we do not know how it might occur, or when, for ourselves or others, but we *know* it will. I am grateful that my expiration date has not yet been reached nor, obviously, has yours, given that you're still reading…

Although I do try to be aware each day, living life as fully as I can with what is in front of me, I am equally aware of how I often slip out of that awareness to where I am simply not fully present. A simple example is how I often catch myself driving like a robot while my thoughts are elsewhere.

A major area in which we lose our focus on the present comes from the stories we make up around fear—fear of what could happen; fear of all of the what-ifs we create. They immediately take us out of the here and now. I love the profound statement read by Franklin D. Roosevelt in his inaugural address: "The only thing we have to fear is fear itself." If the tiger is not in front of us, how can we fear the tiger? It is only because, in our minds, we have created the story that the tiger is coming, even though there is nothing in our reality at that moment to indicate anything about a tiger or indeed the future.

Nevertheless, we allow fear to run our lives. What if the market collapses? What if my partner falls in love with someone else? What if I lose my job? What if I make the wrong choice? The list is endless. We give away our energy to something that has not happened—that we don't even know will ever happen—rather than being focused on what *is* happening. Only the mind can create the story that brings forward the illusion of fear. Even though I know this well, and no longer get so pulled in by fear, I can still find myself caught up in my self-created story about what could happen tomorrow. Yet *the future never comes.*

Along with getting caught up in the future, we avoid being fully available to this day by holding on to energies from the past. How many stories in your life will you not let go of? What resentments have you not cleared up? Using the analogy of the 86,400 seconds that accompany each day, a young man from Harlem made a video about how to live life. How do you spend each second of your life? Another useful analogy: we wake up with $100 worth of energy every morning. How are we going to spend our gift today? The past is the past, whether it be a fraction of a second ago or ten years ago—it is all the same. The minute our minds dredge up a story from the past, we are using some of that valuable $100 worth of energy that was our gift upon waking this morning. Anything other than this present moment uses some of the energy money, so of course we have less energy for today. This could translate out to our physical bodies in the form of tiredness, muscle ache, or depression.

My brother hung on for over twenty years to a resentment about a comment I had made regarding an event with our father. He felt I had lied about what had happened whereas my point of view was not that. He changed our family dynamics through his resentment, and caused stress for my mother, who was always trying to resolve the issue. More importantly, his holding on as he did cost him energy every time he went back into his story about what I had done to him. Our two perceptions of the incident were clearly different, and he would not consider shifting his. Through self-exploration, I reached the place where I could sincerely appreciate his perspective, which, in turn, gave me empathy and compassion along with understanding for his reactivity. I would occasionally call him, just to let him know I was thinking of him, and eventually when he was nearing his death (although he was not conscious of just how close it was) he began to soften toward me. A few weeks prior to him dying instantly—as in drop-dead instant—he even cried on the phone as he shared with me how current changes in his life were affecting and disturbing him. From my end, I was so very glad I had made that last call to him. And I wonder now if he had softened because he had an unconscious knowing he was going to die.

Some friends of mine have a similar kind of situation. The whole family loved each other's company, and you would call them a close family. One day, however, one sister made a comment to another sister regarding an event in her immediate family. Many years later, the sister who continues to feel "harmed," (whom we will call the "victim" for ease of identification) still refuses to forgive her sister (the "offender") who made the comment. As a consequence, the offender sister has not only been ostracized from the family, but it is also understood that no one else in the family will have any form of contact with her. The close relationships she had had with the rest of the family have been destroyed. Though the others had nothing to do with the incident, because the victim sister refuses to forgive unless there is an apology from the offender, there can be no contact between them. A simple apology won't do; instead it must be a "taking back of all the words" that the offender uttered. Looking deeper, one could say that the victim, through refusing to forgive, is holding the rest of the family hostage through control. "If so-and-so comes to the party, I will not," she said. Choices then have to be made, even though the others are not involved in the conflict. Both offender and victim are equally pained by this cutting-off and the splintering of the family dynamics. In my experience, suffering is stored in the body and may well manifest in some physical form, such as an illness. Imagine the tremendous waste of life-giving energy expended in holding on to such a story.

When we hold on to such a story, we are saying someone harmed us. The "how" doesn't matter, it is all the same. The story can be recreated only through memory—the thoughts are all from the past and have emotions attached to them. Forgiveness in the Judeo-Christian paradigm is based on: "You did something to me, but I'm now going to forgive you for having harmed me." True forgiveness, on the other hand, has absolutely nothing to do with the other person. Consider this powerful quote by Lewis B. Smedes: "To forgive is to set a prisoner free and discover that the prisoner was you."

As with anything in life that pushes our buttons and causes a reaction ("I will not speak to you again until you apologize!"), the underbelly is ours and *ours alone*. Our suffering is self-imposed, because no one can harm us or make us feel any way, about anything. Our mind creates the story, and as long as the story gets repeated and held on to, there can be no resolution.

For some of you, your mind is going into over-drive defending against what I've just said. "Of course it was her fault!" you might say. "She *did* hurt me when she lied, and made me look incapable and stupid."

Although I am no longer coming from any religious paradigm, I do like the parable of Christ in which he says: "He that is without sin among you, let him first cast a stone at her." (John 8:7) In other words, have you always been perfect? Have you never done or said something that you wish you hadn't? Have you never had a "bad" thought that you would dread anyone finding out about? Are you so perfect that you can stone others to death in self-righteous indignation? This is exactly what we are doing when we are in the place of judging someone, whether it's something they said or something they did.

The reality is that no matter who says or does what, not until there is recognition of our own humanness and, through that, our acceptance of another's humanness, can there be resolution. Simply put, dropping the story and being in the present clears the slate. The spiritually mature person can do that, the spiritually immature child cannot. Earlier in this chapter I shared how I remind myself that I could be dead tomorrow. From that, the question we have to ask ourselves whenever we are in conflict with someone is: "If this were the last day of my life, would I want to die holding on to this resentment?"

A friend had just come back from an extended trip, arriving only the day before an event she had planned prior to leaving. The event included tickets—for herself, her husband, her brother, and his wife—to a concert. Each of them had loved the musical group's performances for years, so it was a particularly special evening. They had a lively dinner, talking about the trip and other events, before heading for the concert.

The brother of my friend dropped the three of them at the door and went to park the car. When the concert was about to start, the brother still hadn't come to the seats. His wife got up to look for him, only to find paramedics trying to save him after he had collapsed at the top of the stairs coming into the theatre. In his mid-50s, he had died instantly.

Although this is a particularly poignant and tragic story, it is also a variant of one we hear time and again. We might allow ourselves to experience our feelings on hearing of such instant death, yet we quickly lose our moment of awareness of our own mortality. The mind plays its games and in some odd, perverse way manages to make the mortality everyone else's except ours. I am often aware of this with myself, and I also quickly forget. More than the fear of our own mortality, what is it? What happens that makes us want to shut out the rising emotions, those unpleasant feelings, and shove them deep inside ourselves? Is it our own vulnerability, our feeling that if we allow ourselves to fully feel what something could mean in our lives, that we will be overcome with emotion? I often see, in working with people, that there can be an unconscious fear of allowing an emotion to take over. No emotion will kill you, although I know it can certainly feel as though it will. That fear of the power of the emotion is enough to stop us. Yet the stuffing away tends to raise its demanding head in another way, another time, and, if unaddressed, can lead to the person becoming emotionally shut down.

So now you may understand why I do my best to live today as though it could be my last. The mantra at the head of this chapter propels me to be vulnerable: to let you read these experiences of my life. Perhaps in reading, you will deepen your willingness to live today rather than yesterday or tomorrow. Remember, life is not a dress rehearsal.

As Eleanor Roosevelt famously said: "Yesterday is history, tomorrow is a mystery, and today is a gift; that's why they call it the present."

CHAPTER THREE:

Life Unfolds in Spite of Us

We are really not human beings on a spiritual journey but rather, spiritual beings on a human journey.

Pierre Teilhard de Chardin, French philosopher, priest

Each morning before getting out of bed, I offer my thank you to the Divine for experiencing another sunrise. In Pooh language, it is my favorite day because I am alive! All on its own, life is a precious gift.

I marvel so at the unfolding of life—the magic, the unpredictable, the unchangeable. As I take you on my journey, we will explore how we can participate more in life, through increasing our awareness of experiences, thereby shifting out of patterns and habitual repetitive actions. Although life appears to be in charge of what is put in front of us, at the same time it seems that through increased awareness we can shift how we respond to our experience.

A close friend of mine was going for a long weekend of guys' golf. Several of them were on the same flight, during which one almost 50-year-old guy had a severe seizure and stopped breathing. *As it so happened*, he was sitting next to a physician, who saved his life. Had that not been the case, by the time a physician had been located on board and been able to attend to him, most likely he would have died. No physician at all on board would probably have meant imminent death.

When we hear of such events, and in our desire to make some sense out of them, we often use expressions such as "fortunate," "lucky," "by chance," and "coincidence," rather than dropping into the awesomeness, using the opportunity to marvel at the magic and the mystery of our lives unfolding. Conventional wisdom might say, "It seems it just wasn't his time." And so Who or What controls when it is—or isn't—the time for our final curtain?

It then *just so happened* that because I had left my friend a phone message, he returned my call after dealing with the paramedics on arrival at the group's destination. I had received disconcerting news from my doctor just a few hours earlier that had left me feeling quite fragile, and I was wanting to share it with those close to me. His call was perfectly timed.

For the most part, I live my life spontaneously rather than what others might term logically or prudently. When I want to make light of my apparent lack of logical reasoning for my actions, I often humorously use my personal mantra of "I could be dead tomorrow" as my excuse. Yet that is the literal truth: I could be dead tomorrow, as could any of us. On that particular day, however, I had received information about serious medical markers that indicated something was going on in my physical body that needed to be investigated. The translation of the medical information left me with the stark realization that, truly, I could drop dead from either a heart attack or a stroke.

Wow! The news was akin to a 100,000-volt jolt as the black head of fear rose immediately from my inner depths. It was astonishing to see the effect this had on me, the one who frequently says: "I could be dead tomorrow." That expression had now switched from a light and flippant saying to a potentially imminent truth. It was then, as I was sitting at home contemplating the information I had just received, that my friend called. What a great gift it was for me, hearing the story from him about his friend at just this time. I was being reminded yet again, just as we all are being reminded every day, of the great life mystery over which we are not in control and cannot change. Looking back on our lives, we can see how it all appears like a well-written play while at the same time containing events we could not possibly take credit for having created.

So, like Pooh, live today as though this is your last, and one day it will be. Yes, one day my life-movie will end and it will be my last day on planet Earth.

Throughout the years, I've been encouraged by many people of various sorts, from professionals to friends, to write about my life experiences—what they have meant to me, how one significant event effortlessly leads into the next. I have also known myself that I needed to do this, yet I kept putting it off, for a variety of reasons. Now, however, having been reminded in this poignant manner that tomorrow is not guaranteed, I no longer could put off my writing.

"If not now, when?" was suddenly in my face. I had to acknowledge to myself how, rather than being willing to feel uncomfortable about writing my story for others to read, I had always found reasons to not even get started. Clearly, I was not following my own wisdom—not walking my talk. When teaching, I would often use as my last slide: "Free Drinks Tomorrow." I love the powerful simplicity of this little dynamite phrase just as much as the first time I saw it. Yup. Free drinks tomorrow means you could drink freely then, yet many people miss the point that tomorrow truly never ever comes. It is always just today. It is only ever now. It is our minds that attempt to hold on to past stories or create future plans. So if you have something you've been wanting to do, or if you've been waiting to see someone you want to see, or if there is something you need to say to someone that you've been holding on to, then I say: today is all you have. What have you been putting off doing until tomorrow? Listen to your answer!

Our truth and wisdom can come only from our experiences. There can be no truth or wisdom if I tell you of someone else's experiences. Yet I can be willing to share my life stories with you and, in this way, perhaps stir up some memory of your own. From the seeing of life just as it is, without a need to change it, without resistance to that which is, comes freedom. How about it? Are you into flying on the wings of freedom, released from the illusionary chains of limitations you've been told all your life you have? I hope so!

Let's start with what I mean by the word "freedom." Freedom, in my language, is about living daily from a place of contentment, ease, peace, and joy rather than conducting your life according to what you've been told you can or cannot or have to or must do. Living freely encompasses seeing life as it is— whatever is in front of you at this moment, without resistance, and without the need to make it something else or something different. Freedom is moving out of "Should-Ville" into "Alive-Ville!"

The kind of freedom I'm addressing doesn't come from gathering more information or adding concepts from an ever-expanding list of teachers and books; nor does it come from the learning of anything. Indeed, on the contrary, breaking through the clouds into flying high and free, with the internal long-distance vision of an eagle, comes from an *un-learning* of everything you've been told is true. As a client said: "I don't want to take any more workshops of any kind. I don't want to read more books or listen to more CDs of people telling me what to do or what *their* life is. I want movement in my own life and now, doing this work, for the first time this is exactly what I am getting."

So now, answer as honestly as you can: How are you with your life? Are you content and at ease with it? What words would you use to describe your life? How much of your life are you wanting to change? Have you been living your unique truth or have you been living according to the rules, regulations, shoulds, and have-tos—set up by others—that you have been told are your truths? Are you living your life for you or for others? If you dare to allow yourself to feel, do you feel full or empty inside? Do you see your glass of life as half full or half empty?

Being honest with yourself in answering these questions may perhaps leave you feeling a bit shaken. Indeed, if we're living our life for others and society, according to their rules, it's likely that we don't really want to question it. We don't want to hear our own answer, therefore we deem it best not to ask. For many, maintaining a comfortable status quo, not rocking the boat, not even allowing the questioning, is preferable because even the possibility of change can be terrifying. Yet if we really want to begin to feel glorious, free-flying freedom, such honest self-introspection is mandatory. You can't get there any other way for the very simple reason that this is all about you finding *your* truth, the truth that belongs to you alone. Your truth that comes from inside and not from outside. Your truth that comes from you alone and not from someone else telling you your truth.

It's very simple: *your* truth comes from *your* experience and not from someone else's experience. That is your only truth, and anything outside of your direct experience is an *un-truth*. How can it be otherwise?

I am writing here about my experiences and how life unfolding has shown me its magic. In telling you intimate pieces of my life and sharing what insights I have had from them, I hope you will be inspired to look at your own life with equal awe as you begin to see your guiding Grace.

Is there a bridge between my reality and yours? It would seem there is, certainly in part, although most definitely we never see the same situation with the same eyes. Eyewitness accounts, for example, no longer carry the power punch in court, because it has been shown in multiple studies just how different each person's report is of the same incident. We experience everything in life through one or more of our senses: we see, hear, taste, smell, and touch our experiences, and these then become our filters and conditioned responses. Our very first infant experience begins to lay the foundation for similar experiences, building on that initial one and resulting in the layering of filters. Each filter is added to, resulting in myriad layers. Our *unique* filters now become like colored glasses that, in turn, determine our reactions or responses to life. It is our perception, through these layered filters, that gives us our particular point of view. What we experience through our unique filters becomes what we call our reality. Indeed, we believe that this is in fact reality, period.

You may have heard this joke before, but it's worth telling again. There's a Buddhist monk in New York who operates a hotdog stand. A guy comes up, hands the monk a twenty-dollar bill, and says, "Make me one with everything."

Cute, huh? But there's more. The monk puts the twenty dollars in his cash box and then hands the guy his loaded hotdog. "Hey, where's my change?" he asks. Sweetly, the monk replies, "Ahhhhh, change comes from within!"

So this is simply about *you* looking internally at *your life*, seeing for yourself who you are and are *not*, and through this, finding *your own unique truth*. It requires nothing less than an honest willingness to explore yourself, to question that what you say, is. It has nothing to do with anyone telling you what you need to do in order to find your truth. No one can tell you your truth—that belongs solely to you. Once this simple step is taken, you are granted freedom to live life un-encumbered by the rules and regulations of the shoulds, have tos and musts that have been imposed on you by others.

The title of this chapter is a powerful piece of understanding: *Life unfolds in spite of us*. This statement no longer holds any debate for me; rather, through my life experiences, it has become a knowing. And this knowing has come through my willingness to be brutally honest with myself, having nothing to do with thinking through to a conclusion or any attempted logic through discussion. Knowing, unlike information or having knowledge, comes from the heart, which is why we say, "I know it by heart" or "I know it in my heart."

Nevertheless, I do remember the times of many juicy, often highly emotional and endless unsolvable discussions, when this knowing was far from my reality. For years I was caught up in life, in survival mode, just coping. My spiritual path and exploring of philosophy were put on the back burner from age 20 until I really had no other choice, years later, than to delve into my inner life. That was when life showed me, in no uncertain terms, that enough was enough and it was time to get back to what was really important. Yet, paradoxically, even while I was ignoring my inner life for many years, I nevertheless knew, from an early age, that my life truly does unfold in spite of me, even if I didn't use those words.

I seem to have been born with an innate trust of life that also translated to trust of people. My mother was always displeased about this aspect of me, and often admonished me for it. When I would say something to the effect that I knew my trusting such and such a person was okay, her irritation with me was obvious with her sarcastic question: "Oh and just how is it that you know?" Yet even as early as age three, I would answer, "I don't know, I just know." Nowadays, I am empathic to her natural mother's concern and protectiveness, which came out in sarcasm rather than facing her fears for me.

"Trust" might not be as clear a word to use here as "intuition," and actually I prefer to say it's a trusting intuition that I've always had. I daresay most children have these same types of intuitive experiences. Unfortunately, when children express what they're feeling, these feelings are generally negated or undermined in some way by the parent. Yet the natural state for children is an intuitive, curious, non-judgmental one—until, that is, the light gets slowly snuffed out as the children begin to take on the beliefs that others are imposing on them.

As I look back, I see how my spontaneity, which I love and which has been a wonderful life gift, comes from my continuing trusting nature. Nevertheless, even though I have had this natural intuitive trust for what life puts in front of me, I have also argued violently with life at various times. I have been angry with life. I have tried to control life. I have damned "God" for what's in front of me, and I have insisted I do indeed have at least some control. In the end, however, after struggling with the need to be right and suffering what comes with that, I could find nothing left to argue with. So surrender happened.

Surrender is a releasing of the holding on to the illusion that we have control; it is a feeling of powerlessness. Paradoxically, surrendering to powerlessness leads to personal power. Surrender, however, cannot be forced. Go ahead: just try saying "I surrender" ten thousand times and see for yourself if that leads to your surrender to whatever is in front of you. No! Surrender just happens. Surrender can happen only as our understanding forms from having the willingness to open to the exploration of self, to walk the burning coals, and to see our own patterns and the roots of our beliefs. Only when we reach the place of some understanding can surrender begin to unfold.

When I could finally surrender, the truth of *my* experience was clear: Life does unfold in spite of me.

I mentioned that I knew the truth of this from an early age, so let me tell you now about my very first experience that I can remember. This is something that has stayed with me all my life, and if I go to this memory, I feel once again how I felt and see it all as clearly as then. I was only about six months old. Yes, that's right, I am saying I remember a particular scene in my life from when I was only about six months of age. Although I could stand up, I needed to be holding onto something, which is why I'm saying "about six months." I am standing in my crib, hanging onto the rail, with my little legs wobbling in their effort to keep me upright. I can hear my mother coming down the hall and I am looking straight at the door, waiting for her to open it. As she opens the door, my thought is, "Uh-oh! What did I get myself into this time?" Obviously I didn't have this language at the time, yet nevertheless this was the energy and those were my internal words. How does an infant of such a young age remember anything? Yet, as I've said, this is a memory that has been with me all my life. Is it true? If you find yourself wanting to make some judgmental or dismissive comment, ask yourself first, can you possibly know it is not true? This can become a valid form of questioning for you as you explore.

Therefore, throughout this book, I will continually refer you to yourself for your own self-examination. Nothing I say is true for anyone other than me. I am not telling you this is how something is or is not. I merely want to act as a pointer of sorts, to prod and poke a bit, to provoke you, to lead you into examining the unfolding of your life, and thus seeing the perfection of it in remembering your truth from your experience.

I was a frustration for my mother in so many ways, as you'll see. It was only in later years that I could feel true compassion for her, in seeing how I was the trigger of so much of her suffering. My mother was a wonderful person, loved by almost anyone who knew her throughout her long life. She loved me as a mother, yet her driving need was that she wanted me to be what she wanted me to be, and that was according to the ideology, images, and beliefs she held. She was going to be a "good" mother no matter what, and raise me to behave the way I "'was supposed to" so that she, in turn, would be seen as having done a good job as my mother in raising me. As a consequence, because I did not follow her blueprint, she suffered a lot. As with the intuitive trust issue, throughout my life my mother had difficulty accepting me as me, and my behavior.

Various early childhood experiences combined to begin the formation of beliefs I've held all my life around feeling as if I didn't belong. I felt as though I had been born into the wrong family, though there was never any question my parents were my biological parents. The following is an event I also vividly recall—another that has stayed with me all my life, like the crib incident— adding to the sense of separation and loneliness I used to feel. To understand this timeframe, let me say that this was long before any talk of space travel. Any mention or even the possibility of "life out there" or "aliens" was simply not a point of discussion. Generally, people were conservative in their thoughts about our universe, never mind the cosmos, assuming that Earth was the only inhabited planet. Certainly any type of space conversation would never have been a topic in my home nor among my parents' friends, meaning that I did not get any of what I am about to say from overhearing adults talk.

My parents, brother, and I were outside on a clear summer night. Although we were in the city, the stars were brightly visible. My birthday is in May and I had just turned four. I remember we had all been looking up at the sky when I said: "Where *is* everyone else?" My mother was horrified. "Where *do* you get these *crazy* ideas?" she curtly asked. "What are you talking about? No one lives out *there!*" My brother, nine years my senior, made some belittling comment while agreeing with my mother. I remember how very alone I felt right then. How was it that they didn't know there really *are* others living "out there?" As with my crib incident, although I was still too young to have the language skills to be able to express this, I just couldn't understand how grown-ups didn't understand something that was so obvious to me.

If you happen to be someone who has a closed-door belief about even the possibility of life elsewhere, I again ask you simply: "Do you know it to be true that there is no life in other parts of the cosmos?" If you can't answer from your knowing, then it remains an unanswerable question and open to possibility.

Have you ever looked back on events in your life where, as a kid, you just knew what you knew, as in the above examples where it had nothing to do with someone else telling me anything? One of the biggest disservices, from generally well-meaning parents, is when children are belittled for their unique creative expressions. "That's just your crazy imagination!" or simply "Stop imagining such things" are certainly phrases I heard. Yet I ask you, what is the difference between creative inspiration and imagination? Isn't it really that one is acceptable while the other is not?

So before I even hit grade one, my mother was wondering what was wrong with me. I imagine she was hoping the nuns at St. John's Catholic School would straighten me out so I would behave as I was supposed to. Alas, this next period of my life would just add to her sorrow. You can read more about this in the chapter *God Doesn't Care What You Wear*. For the moment, though, before I move on to the formation of our beliefs, let me tell you of an incident that, for me, illustrates what I have already said about your truth being unique to you and coming from your experience.

Although I was raised as a Catholic and attended Catholic schools throughout my schooling (prior to university), I have not belonged to a religion since age 20. Religion, for me, does not equal my own connection to a higher power, be it called The Divine, God, Spirit, Source, or whatever name that attempts to name that which cannot be named. On the other hand, my spiritual life, which I define as my self-exploration to know myself, has been my priority for many years now. Throughout my life, there just seemed to be a driving force that had me ponder beliefs so that, from the beginning of my schooling, I was filled with questions. As a small child of six, studying catechism as we did every morning in the Catholic school, I had question after question in my effort to understand. One morning, the nun was talking about Heaven in a very flavorful way, describing the peace of being there and of the love of God and Jesus while being with all your family who died before you. The key imagery she presented was of a kindly older man—that would be God—taking care of everyone and everything, having created a pure paradise for all to enjoy. That is, provided you were Catholic! (Only Catholics go to Heaven, didn't you know that?) As a little kid, listening intently about this idyllic Heaven and feeling excited, I raised my hand, waving it for immediate attention. "Yes," said the nun, "what is your question?" with more than a slight irritation to her voice for having been interrupted while declaring such a major truth. From a place of pure child innocence, I breathlessly asked, "Oh, sister, sister, have you been there?!" The nun, being more than a little upset because, clearly, she was not able to honestly and truthfully answer "yes" to what I had asked, instead gave me the razor strap in front of the class. Was the nun speaking *her* truth or was she simply parroting what she had been told? Given that she hadn't gone to Heaven and come back, the answer is obvious. Yet, as we'll see, this illustration of *un-truth* is not any different from all of our beliefs that we believe to be so true, thus allowing them to shape our lives.

CHAPTER FOUR:

The World According to Shakespeare...or, your life-movie

Accept, then act. Whatever the present moment contains, accept it as if you had chosen it. Always work with it, not against it. This will miraculously transform your whole life.

Eckhart Tolle

Shakespeare, in his play *As You Like It*, says: "All the world's a stage, and all the men and women merely players. They have their exits and their entrances, and one man in his time plays many parts." And so it is. I see my life as a movie in which I am the main character, while you may be one of the other characters. I may also be a character in your movie, but my movie is about me and your movie is about you. It seems we meet when one of us is in the next scene for the other.

In order for you or anyone else to see the genius of your own life unfolding, simply take the time to reflect. I'm certainly not here to say that this is the way it is about anything, because it's your movie, in which you are the main character while the other characters come and go, depending on what part of your movie they are in. It's just about being willing to look with courageous self-honesty, digging deeper, taking in the bigger picture. See how one event in your life led into the next event, in spite of you.

How many times have you heard an inexplicable story, the awesome kind that leaves you with a comment such as, "How in the world did that happen?" Yet we all know, when these events occur there was nothing anyone or any force could have done to change the event. The Yemenia Airline crash in 2009 off the east coast of Africa in which hundreds of people lost their lives, with the only survivor being a young child, is an example of what I'm talking about. No person could have saved the child because there was no one around—the child was simply saved from the crash and found on rescue. To try and answer "How?" or "Why?" would be useless. *It just happened*; it just was.

The incredible photos and video from early 2013 of the over 10,000 ton meteorite racing across the Russian skies before smashing into Earth with a force of thirty atomic bombs is a brilliant illustration of life happening without anyone's participation in where the event will occur or indeed the happening of the event itself. I daresay we do not have the power, not our earthly power at least, to do a single thing about such an event—not to change it, to alter it, or even to determine its potential. Although all this may seem humorous or blatantly obvious, we nevertheless seem to forget very quickly, after such reminders, that we're not in charge of life's unfolding, and we continue to live life as though the opposite were true, as if our personal control does exist.

Yet we receive amazing assistance in a continuous attempt to remind us that we quite simply are not in charge. Remember in 1998 when the Swissair flight 111 went down off the coast of Nova Scotia, killing all 229 on board? What struck me most upon hearing of this tragedy was the incredible dance of this happening. It seems that a Divine point wanted to be made by choosing something that *shouldn't* have happened. After all, Swissair, at the time, was considered the safest airline in the world, with a flawless safety record. So when the flight went down, the impact was far greater than if it had been, for example, Aeroflot, known at the time for its lack of safety.

Still, the human mind has a very short memory when it comes to such point-
ers. We forget these reminders of the Mystery and our powerlessness because
it's just too prickly and uncomfortable to feel powerless. I imagine we also
forget because if we haven't started to seriously examine life from this broader
perspective—noting the unfolding that occurs clearly without our help, negat-
ing control on our part— it just seems too big. So instead we do everything
to keep ourselves in the small illusion of feeling powerful. We reach for words
and images in an attempt to describe and explain our world. Our minds search
for the correct answer so that then we can feel safe in believing we have some
control. As the teacher Adyashanti succinctly says: "every instant arises completely on its own, without an explanation."

Many years ago I had some T-shirts made with slogans on them that I sold.
Probably the most popular, and certainly my favorite, was: "Wanna' Make God
Laugh? Tell 'Em Your Plans!"

"So let me get this straight," you ask. "You're telling me, Life unfolds in spite
of me? So you're trying to make me believe that I'm not in charge, that I don't
have *any* control, ever, over my life?"

Well, let me ask you this: if you've ever had any measure of control, why
wouldn't you have control over everything in your life all the time? In other
words, if you ever had control, why would you have given it up?

When I was studying to teach an advanced module of The BodyTalkSystem
that included the issue of personal control, I began to seriously ask myself some
questions—like the question of having control some of the time. Pondering and
pondering, arguing various other points, I eventually came to the ridiculously
simple and only answer there could be. Once this happened, I sat by myself and
belly laughed and laughed at the understanding of how control is a moot point,
nothing more than an illusion.

I imagine you immediately want to argue with me, and that's cool. You
decide for yourself. Here was my realization: If I tell you I'm in control, which
means you cannot be in control, what would be your response? If I'm in control,

then doesn't that mean that every other person on planet Earth is under, or dictated to, by my control? Fun, don't you think? Control is an absolute, just like pregnancy. Can you be half-pregnant? No, of course not. You're either pregnant or you're not. And, again, if you have had control at any time, why would you have ever given it up? More fun! Recent mainstream scientific research is showing that the Universe is a pre-determined mechanism, down to the smallest detail, such as what you eat for lunch (albeit we still want to think we choose our lunch).

When I look back on my life's unfolding, I am able to see the perfection of how one event led into the next major event, that led into the next major event, and so on. I know of no one who has done this exercise who has not been able to see the various acts of their life-movie in this way. Often the event is the meeting of a particular person that led to you meeting someone else, that led to a particular event. It has been through this reflection, looking back on significant times of my life, that I have come to the place where I say this statement with a knowing—not a piece of knowledge that someone told me, but rather with an internal knowing. Only you can look for your own magical unfolding and in doing so see the guidance of Grace.

I have been gifted with many people coming into my life in the form of teachers, yet in the end *life* has been my best teacher. Divine Presence and Grace have always been there for me and for you, even if we haven't always been consciously aware of them. My task has been, and is, to pay attention, to notice, and to be aware as often as I can be. Yet it's comforting to know that Divine Guidance is here, even if I am not paying attention.

At a popular helicopter ski lodge in the mountains of western Canada, the skiers were chatting gaily about the great conditions while enjoying lunch. When it was time for the next ride, they all piled outside with their gear and climbed into the waiting helicopter. Then, just as they were getting ready for takeoff, one of the skiers announced that he didn't feel like doing that run and got off. The helicopter crashed during its climb to the mountain ridge, and all on board were killed. Although this skier may not have been consciously aware, he nevertheless received and acted on internal Divine Guidance. It would appear that it was not his time to depart this life.

An internal voice is my Divine Guidance, which leads the way for me whether I am listening or not. Albeit unconsciously, I seem to act from that voice, the internal messenger, much of the time, although often the insight about the action I've taken comes only when I look back. In the present moment, my action is simply my response to what is in front of me, without analysis. Yet the more I have examined my past, and acknowledged the guidance that has been offered, the more I have developed a term of reference, an experience to feel back into. Having terms of reference allows for an increasing awareness, which in turn allows us to shift away from the analysis and dissection of why we should or should not do something, and into that simple action response instead.

There was a Canadian fellow, Brian Clark, in one of the towers during the 9/11 event in 2001 in New York. Although the megaphones were shouting for people to go up, saying that the way down was blocked, Brian was going down. There was a bit of an argument between him and some of the people he met in the stairwell, who were telling him he needed to turn around. They were going up as they had been told to do, while he was following what felt right for him. At this point, Brian heard a cry for help, which took his attention away from the disagreement to following the sound. He found the man who was yelling, named Stanley Praimnath, and helped him out of the debris. They continued going down. They were two of only four people who survived the towers from above the impact. Later, when interviewed, Brian said what he learned from this incident was that you know nothing about the next minute, so therefore be in the moment and enjoy it. His life script just happened to include Divine Grace leading him out of the chaos to survival.

In a photo, a cleaning lady is shown being helped by a fireman as she escapes one of the towers just before it crumbles. She said later in an interview how her life had changed dramatically following that event. Literally two months later she was killed in the American Airlines crash in Queens, New York. Simply put, her expiration date hadn't yet been reached two months earlier.

One of the more profound ways I notice my life unfolding in spite of me is through the people I have met, leaving me with a deep gratitude for every person who has been a part of my life. We wonder, of course, how it is we have met those who have influenced us and why. Well, as I see it, it's like when we're in a huge shopping mall. There are thousands of people there, just as there are billions in the world. When I'm in the mall, of course I notice people. I might see some good-looking guys, maybe dressed in snazzy Italian clothes. I might notice a mother who is afraid yet appears angry with her child. I might pass someone and feel their grief. So I notice various people and aspects of them, as I imagine is also your experience.

That is very different from when someone grabs my attention, when my attention is being drawn to a person. Out of these thousands upon thousands I may encounter, very few people will draw me in—very few will be an actor in my life-movie. Yet it is clear how each one who has been a significant player in my life has arrived, according to plan, to be a part of my Divine movie. It is through looking back at how specific actors have come into a scene of my movie—some staying for only one scene, others staying for many—that I am struck by the perfection of the script. I could not have written the script nor predicted the next scene.

Going back to the quote from Shakespeare at the beginning of this chapter, I also see my life as having a script that is being played out in my movie. The world is my stage. My perceived reality appears to unfold as each part of the script that is written unfolds. Interestingly, most religions have a saying that encompasses: "And so it is." Yes, and so it is. Amen.

When I am giving my point of view on this subject, I use the analogy of my life being a journey from point A to point B. Regardless of what I do, I know I will get to point B when I get to point B, and not a moment before. Let's stop for a minute here and just observe point B, which is when we cease to have our physical existence. The final curtain of the movie comes down. We die. If you want to see how much control you have, just try and change someone's death! You can have the best-educated physicians in the world and the most power-ful healers all trying to keep someone alive, and if it is the person's time to exit their movie, they die. You cannot stop the process no matter how much you may want to keep the person's physical body functioning. Conversely, there are many documented incidences in which a person who has been declared medically dead yet kept alive on life support, when removed from the support system continues to survive, often for a considerable time as in months and even years. Then when it is the end of their story, they die. We come into this life through our first breath, and we leave with our last breath. Our grandmothers, and I imagine their grandmothers, would have said: "When it's your time, it's your time and not before." They said this because it was their observation, just as I imagine many of us may agree from our own observations of the same.

My mother, in her nineties and seemingly at peace with leaving, used to say, "I guess it's just not my time yet." And so it wasn't. At the beginning of one September, I had planned my day to include going to the farmer's market, running a couple of errands, and then seeing my mother later in the day. But, as I was getting myself ready in the morning, it became clear to me—an internal message—that I needed to go and see my mother first before doing anything else. She was weeks shy of her 93rd birthday and living alone in a care facility for seniors in her own apartment. When I got to her door, I tried to see if it was locked and it wasn't. As I went in, calling out to her, there was no answer. I found my mother in bed, completely unresponsive to my voice, and from what I could tell, in a coma. When the ambulance arrived, the staff quickly saw she was indeed in a coma, and at the hospital it was determined the coma was brought on by glucose-deprivation. Now, with this type of coma, there are two normal outcomes. If the patient does come out of the coma, there will most likely be decreased mental capabilities, usually severe because of the brain having been deprived for a period of time of its vital glucose. The second outcome, and the most common, is death.

My mother came out of her coma after several days, and within a few more was completely back to her previous state. Adding a touch of levity, she had always said to me, with a threatening humorous tone in her voice, that if she ever ended up in the hospital I was to promise that I would get her false teeth back in immediately. With the help of a nurse, we were able to get her teeth in just as she was beginning to come out of the coma. When she was only barely conscious and still not able to speak, one of the first things she did was to check her mouth to make sure her teeth were in. As best she could, she mumbled a grateful "Thank you."

It just so happened that the head of Internal Medicine and I had chatted and hit it off, so he took it upon himself to come by a couple of times a day. He kept saying to me that I mustn't expect my mother to live, that it would be only a matter of days before she died. Finally, however, he admitted that, although from the medical perspective she was expected to die, my mother had turned out to be a perfect example of how we can never know what will happen, even when we think we know. At that point, he said he would arrange for a hospice and *it just so happened* that the first one to have a vacancy was only minutes from my home, allowing me to visit my mother every day. Although she was never able to get out of bed on her own again, my mother went on to live for another three months and three weeks, during which she was totally lucid. In her words, "I haven't lost a marble!" Then, with a laugh, she'd add, "I guess St. Peter still doesn't want me yet." She was, after all, Catholic! This miraculous gift of "extra" time, from her coma up to her death, allowed for healing: tenderness and expressions of gratitude and goodbyes from and for my mother, for myself, and for everyone in the family. Although she didn't speak of a near-death experience, something had happened to my mother when she was in the coma. When she regained consciousness, there was an obvious shift. She no longer had any fear about anything, and she was more present than I had ever experienced her before. When someone lives a successful life of 93 years, they have already said goodbyes to many of their friends. Nevertheless, my mother had an abundance of visitors. She loved the attention she received from everyone, including the staff that thought of her as their mascot. The nurses, who are really angels wearing nurses' uniforms, would make her comfortable, sitting her up in bed and being sure she had her teeth in and her lipstick on before the first visitor. For myself, these months were a profound gift.

So here we are, back to point B a.k.a. bye-bye for now! As I see it, we all have this journey from point A (coming into life) to point B (exiting). It appears, based on my experience, that we have what I refer to in my work as "detours" along the way—detours of various kinds and lengths and degrees, but in the end, we will all get to point B when it is our time. Do we have a choice along the way as to the length of the detours we encounter? Again, from my experience, although these detours may appear as "choices"—especially because that's how the mind wants to see them—I see them rather as different states of awareness. For example, I may repeat a particular pattern—let's call it a relationship detour—a number of times. Then, through my increasing awareness of the repetition of this pattern, there is a shift in my consciousness so that the next time that particular relationship pattern, or a similar one, shows up, I *choose* not to engage in the pattern. If I do continue to repeat the pattern, instead of noticing and shifting, the same relationship issue will show up, making the detour longer and probably increasingly more painful until I finally *choose* to shift. I still get back on the road from A to B, but with a tortuous detour along the way.

The Buddhists have a great little story about this, which I'll paraphrase here. There is a man who has a habit of going down the same street every day on his way to the market. One day, while walking down this street that he knows well, he falls into a hole. "Oh," he says, "I didn't see that hole!" He pulls himself out, dusts himself off, muttering about how that hole hadn't been there yesterday, and continues on his way. The next day, he repeats the exact same pattern and falls, once again, into the hole. "I forgot about that hole!" The next day, believe it or not, he does the exact same thing again. What a pattern! The fourth day, he turns down this street, but before he gets to the hole, he reminds himself: "Ah, yes, there is a hole there," and he crosses over to the other side of the street. Then on the fifth day, as he's about to turn down this same street, he stops and says, "I think I'll take the next street." If we closely look at our own lives, we can see the holes we keep falling into: our patterns.

So although we will get to point B regardless, given that the human condition seemingly ceases with the death of the physical body, it appears that we can become aware of our patterns and shift our perspective so we go down another street. In other words, with increasing awareness, the detours may not be as long as they once were. Certainly, this has been my own experience.

Let's go back to a particular scene in my life-movie and see the workings of Divine Guidance and Grace. I had been a single parent of two little boys for a couple of years. Anyone who has been down this path knows it can be a challenge, and certainly it was a struggle for me because I received virtually no help—financially or, more importantly, emotionally—from their father. I had not received any financial settlement because he had declared bankruptcy. As a result, I needed to work full time. I made my children their breakfast, left out some things for lunch, and went to work, returning hours after they came home from school. They went to school alone, fortunately only a block away, and were pretty much on their own until I got home at the end of the day, except for when my mother would come by to bring them a treat or check on them. I remember how, in my role as a single mother with the daunting responsibility of being the bread winner, life seemed overwhelming. Yet I couldn't allow myself the luxury of feeling the fear I felt. I remember feeling I would collapse if I let the fear in, and that would be worse. Peeling back the layers, probably my deepest unclaimed fear was that my boys could likely end up in trouble because I wasn't available to them and they had too much unguided time alone.

Then I met someone. It *just so happened* that, at the time, I was working in the consulting business. My boss had organized an international conference for which the keynote speaker was widely known. I wouldn't have met him if it hadn't been for my boss stating that he expected me to attend a cocktail party in honor of this VIP, whom I knew only through his papers and reputation. I hadn't planned on attending the reception because I didn't have a babysitter, nor did I want to spend my few entertainment dollars on meeting someone I had absolutely no interest in knowing. Nevertheless, I heard the unspoken from my boss and knew what it could mean to my job if I didn't attend, so I went. There was a spiral staircase going down to the reception area, which was full by the time I got there. I can clearly remember the blue wool fitted suit I wore that night with a delicious light blue silk blouse tucked in my straight tight skirt, complementing my deep blue eyes and (then) natural blond hair. In those days, I had *very* good legs, which my high heels accentuated as I descended into the room. Of course I was also young! As I was coming down the stairs, I noticed people grouped around this man, giving him their rapt attention, while he visibly lost his attention on them, watching me. He immediately came across the room to where I had entered, introduced himself, and hung around me throughout the evening. My boss now informed me I was to drive this man back to his hotel. That's when

I balked. I smiled sweetly, said I would, and then arranged for several people at the reception to come to my place for an after-party. My intention was then to send this VIP back to his hotel in a cab, alone.

Notice my referring to "I" as though I had anything to do with anything—"I wouldn't have met him," "I hadn't planned on attending"—yet this is how we live our lives, thinking we are in charge.

None of it, of course, turned out as I had thought it would. Rather, life unfolded thereafter in a way I couldn't possibly have orchestrated or controlled. He seriously courted me, which any woman would enjoy. Regardless of his busy schedule, I received several phone calls a day from around the world, and delighted in surprise 24-hour visits with gifts of perfume, champagne, and caviar. For this young woman, it was all intoxicating and irresistible. I didn't know myself well then. I was unaware, unconscious of just how deeply terrified I was of coping with my situation, of my un-allowed fears for myself and my children. When this man showed up as the archetypal "Knight in Shining Armor," it was under the guise of love. The relationship flowered and I capitulated, shoving my doubts deep down.

To my credit, I wanted to do my due diligence so that I would feel as though I was making the "right" decision. I did dig and probe with my questions, wanting to know that what he was telling me was true, but I was just too naïve for the game the big boys play. For example, I asked him one day how old he was. When he told me, I came back with "prove it." I can remember feeling how pro-active I was in asking for such proof, making sure that everything was as it appeared. The age he had told me, of course, matched the passport. How was the then-naïve me to know that this was not his only passport and that his actual age was many years older?

I would spend years blaming him for his lies and deceptions until I was big enough to take on my own self-deception. In being honest with myself, I remember that I knew internally of the lies, yet to admit them would have meant I would have to walk away from this rescue. Instead, I married him and kept my unclaimed information deeply submerged so that I didn't have to know my own lies *nor* myself. Yes, we loved each other, and I thank him for rescuing me and for exposing me to such an expansive life. I was, and remain, extremely grateful for all that he gave my boys. He was a role model in many ways for my sons, and they thought of and loved him as their father. In this scene of my life-movie, and my role in his movie, I also rescued him and became his strongest, most valuable asset. *It just so happened* he had come into my life as I had come into his. I couldn't have planned it.

This relationship gave me the gift of seeing how easily we lie to ourselves and, specifically, how easily I had lied to myself, albeit unconsciously. The dynamic of "The Prostitute" was alive and well, in charge of my world during this phase. When we hear the word "prostitute," most people go to the place of thinking something sexual, yet this archetype has absolutely nothing to do with sex or gender. "The Prostitute" is the energy that happens when we lie to ourselves and sell off a piece of our soul, when we do not live according to our own truth, when we ignore our inner voice. We lie to ourselves many times a day, and some more than others. How often do you do or say something you really don't want to, just because you think you should? We might say something like, "Well, I don't want to hurt her feelings," as a way of not listening to how the soul is asking for a different action. Simple examples: someone might ask you how you are, and you respond with a lie by saying you're great. They ask if you like their outfit, and you say do you when you don't. All this so that the other person doesn't feel uncomfortable. How many times a day do you do a "should" or a "have-to" because you feel it is expected of you? Another common one is when we say, "Oh, we'll have to get together soon," while what we're actually feeling is the exact opposite, and we have no intention of calling the person to do anything. Ordinary everyday white and black lies, suppressing our truth while feeding the hungry Prostitute.

The irony of all this is that when we are true to ourselves we are able to be in love with all those around us and they will feel this love because we will be there in our truth, without the emotional hooks of our lies. In my experience, specifically in working with Brad Blanton, founder of Radical Honesty, people in our lives want honest and real communication rather than our false lies. Even though we may not be conscious of it, on an energetic level lies cut communication, whereas if you give me something of yourself, I feel a connection—I am in touch with you.

As a side-note, being truthful with yourself is an inside job. In other words, this is about becoming self-aware, of noticing what is happening, and claiming it. For example, I might meet someone in the store with whom I'm holding on to some old energy. My job is to notice and acknowledge that I'm perhaps still feeling resentful, let's say. Yet it's not about dumping on someone, telling them how you are resentful. If this is someone in your life, then the place for addressing your resentment isn't in the grocery store, for starters. Regardless of the relationship, as I notice there is a charge for me with this person, simply by noticing it I have now taken away much of the charge. My responsibility is in the noticing what I am feeling. One of the great, simple ways to lift the charge and often to give some lightness is something Arjuna Ardagh uses, which is to say to yourself, "Just like me!" So, let's say there's a party and I'm in a group standing around chatting. A woman friend has turned her seducer-charm up to high, aiming it directly at the men in the group, totally taking over the conversation. Can you see how I've just pointed my finger at her, making her different from me? In fact, I have these very same pieces in me, only, in this moment I am denying them by virtue of the fact that I'm pointing my finger at her. Once I am aware of this piece, I can have internal humor by saying to myself, "Yup, just like me!" In doing this, I am recognizing my seducer; we are the same and there is no separation. As you will see later, there is nothing in you that is not in me, and acknowledging this brings a lightness and often humor to the tension.

From my experience and from watching others, I can see that intimate relationships are often the place where we lie the most. It seems that suppressing the emptiness we feel in the relationship feels much safer than acknowledging it even slightly. In our ego, albeit unconsciously, we are aware on some level that if we face our truth, we will be required to change, often requiring discomfort, and for many people that is simply too much. Change needs to be avoided at all costs, including the cost to our health. Yes, absolutely, relationships along with the unconscious dynamics dictating them can be poisonous and literally killing. When we lie to ourselves, going against our inner knowing, this self-betrayal is energetically stored somewhere in the body. Eventually the stored blocks of energy will manifest, in one physical form or another. Both women and men often stay in a relationship so as not to be alone or to avoid facing their deepest fears, as when I allowed myself to be rescued. Naturally, it can be a comfortable place, knowing we will be taken care of. Often the fear of being able to survive on our own, the sheer terror of feeling unable to cope financially or emotionally, is enough to allow the mind to justify staying in a parasitic relationship. Another common reason for staying is the unexplainable, expressed as: "He's such a nice person and there's nothing wrong with him, it's just that I feel dead in this marriage." The guilt of leaving a relationship for no apparent reason, even though it may be killing you, is enough to stop most people from leaving.

What is often overlooked, because of the hidden fear of possible change, is that working with challenging relationships, bringing self-honesty and vulnerability into the equation, can result in a major shift for the good. Sometimes, although it might mean that the relationship still separates, when it's done from self-honest, open vulnerability rather than finger pointing, there can be healing along with a minimum of damaging fighting—a sharp contrast from many splits. At other times, often when honesty comes forward from both parties in a non-personal and non-blaming manner, the relationship deepens into a mutually nurturing and fulfilling partnership. Both partners find out they're feeling the same way but have been afraid to express it and hurt the other person. Once that's spoken, there's freedom and lightness enabling the now-honest realization to create a juicy relationship. Bringing forward that which is hidden, making it conscious, is the gift; it's the unconscious pieces of us that can be the killers.

Back to this marriage of mine, where eventually the lies in my life could no longer be suppressed no matter how hard I tried. I remember when I knew beyond doubt that the marriage was over. By this time in my life-movie, we had moved to another country. On this particular evening, my husband and I were at a lovely restaurant, eating lovely food and drinking lovely wine. Only there was nothing lovely about it. We were universes apart, and the separation felt unbearable. Unable to be controlled any longer, tears flowed down my face. It was as though some internal tap had been turned on that couldn't be turned off. My husband was mortified and kept whispering at me to stop crying in public. The separation between us had created a huge hole of emptiness in me, and although

I was married, I had never ever felt so alone in my life. I knew then that I could no longer live the lie, and that staying in the lie would have grave consequences for me. Externally, my husband and I were a perfect couple. My life appeared to others as enviable and exciting—Cristal Champagne, chauffeurs, private jets, five-star restaurants, and all that goes with the fast lane. I had absolutely no concerns about money, and although I was not excessive, I was able to buy anything I wanted. So for me to reach the place of deciding to leave was definitely not a comfortable move. Once again, I was terrified. Although this time the terror was greater than when I had suppressed my fear around raising my sons alone, I was also now slightly more conscious of my fear and more trusting that my life was simply unfolding in this way for the next scene.

Before I explain further, I want to place another piece into the mosaic of my magic life guided by Grace. Prior to this dinner of tears, and prior to our move, I had attended medical school for two years. Although I had been passionate about medicine, literally since early childhood, I had given up the idea by quitting university to marry my first husband, the father of my children. (In that era, many people—and that included me—married just to have sex, because pregnancy outside marriage was such a big social stigma.) Many years later, now in medical school, finally doing what I had always wanted, it simply hadn't occurred to me that I might not be able to continue after our move. At this time, there were twelve medical schools in the city, of which eleven had age-limitation policies for women, though not for men. I was given an interview at the one school without the age limitation, in large part because of my husband's influence. The interview took place with three male physicians, including a surgeon. Now we all know that the only way a surgeon is going to make money is to cut. When this surgeon asked me what my views were on preventive medicine, I remember knowing what he wanted me to answer but, instead, out of my mouth came, "For me, sir, prevention is what medicine is really about." The gavel came down and he voted against me. Although this school was now out of the question, from this interview I was granted entrance into another medical school in another city, an hour away by plane. This would have meant my being away from home most of the time while my youngest son was still in school, and I didn't want to leave him. Also, even though I had now come to what was close to a somewhat conscious realization that I was going to leave my marriage, I knew I was not yet ready. And so my medical training ended.

I remember crying for days when I received the rejection letter to that school. My husband was distraught, because any show of emotion was always way too much for him. For me, it seemed the end of my world. Having given up my childhood dream for a man so many years before, and now having been denied the chance to finally do what I had always wanted to do, was devastating for me. What next?

Although it was not possible for me to see beyond my despair at the time, years later I was able to look back on it and be enormously grateful. I imagine my life would look very different had I continued in conventional medicine. As an analytical, prove-it-to-me kind of person then, I don't imagine I would have veered much from the allopathic point of view into integrative medicine, as I was to do later. Beyond any internal doubt, had I continued in conventional medicine, it's highly unlikely I would be writing this book, nor would I know myself as I do and allow myself to be so exposed. For me, as I look back, the perfection of these events leads me to pause and say, yet again, "Thank you."

Let me share another example of how the Universe has supported me and how the magic of every bit of my life-movie could not have been staged by my ego and me. At the time that I applied to continue medical school following our move, we were living in a high-rent brownstone with no thought of buying because the rent was being taken care of by the company. Although it may be difficult to understand, the best way I can describe this to you is to say there was something like a bubbling in me now trying to break through the surface of this yet-unspoken knowing that I would have to leave the marriage. Although I was aware of the growing internal volcano, I kept it suppressed, not yet willing to face what it would mean if I allowed my truth to emerge. I remember how whenever even a small cinder of knowing tried to break through, the fear would show up, smothering the fire inside and paralyzing action. How could I survive on my own, especially now that the opportunity for a medical career was gone? I had no other career. Life would look very different for me if I were on my own, without money and all the comforts. So for then, it was easier to stay where I was than to face the fear.

Before this marriage, when I was still a single parent, my parents had given me a down payment to buy a house, which I had remodeled, increasing its value. When I married this time, I wanted to rent my house out so that I could build some equity of my own. My last husband, however, was completely against the idea and kept at me incessantly to sell. Eventually I was worn down by his insistent logical arguments and gave in, although I did manage to put the money from the sale into my own private account, to which he did not have access. This would be a necessary piece for me later.

Fast forward to the medical school rejection. In stepped my beloved Divine Guidance, showing me what I needed to do that would be another significant piece for me several years later. One morning, shortly after finding out I would not be continuing in medicine, I received a concise and clear internal message: "Prepare yourself for the future. Use your money [from the sale of my previous house] and buy a house." It was so clear that there was not an ounce of question in me. I immediately set about looking at houses to buy. My husband was as against our buying as he had been insistent about my selling, so the tables were turned. I was determined that this was going to happen: we were buying a house, and no objection was going to change this knowing as I set about doing what I needed to do. I was a realtor's nightmare, as I looked at over seventy houses until I found one that felt right. I now agreed to use my money from my previous house to make up half of the down payment, which was the only way my husband would agree, while he put down the other half. Next I set about tearing the insides out of the house and remodeling to increase its value considerably. Using both my money and his, I paid myself nothing for what became a full-time job as the project manager for a year. Our very adequate company rent allowance more than covered the mortgage, meaning that neither of us needed to pay into that and there was a considerable allowance left over. In other words, there was very little actual financial contribution from my husband toward the house, and there was still a gain from the rent allowance.

So the time had come, as had become obvious to me that night in the restaurant, when I could no longer continue in the marriage. I was giving up too much of myself to stay in what was for me a starving, killing relationship. Then one day I received what was another Divinely clear inner message telling me that I was dying: That I would die, literally, physically, if I continued to stay and not listen. I knew this—I simply knew this to be true. I wanted to live, so now there was nothing further I could do but leave the marriage. I made a commitment to myself at that moment, acknowledging that I had indeed heard and that I would take action on what I knew had to be done. My internal bargaining was that I wanted to wait another month or so until the Christmas/New Year season was over. My sons were coming home, friends were also coming to stay with us, and we had a lot of holiday plans.

It just so happened that between making this commitment to myself and my announcing to my husband that I was leaving the marriage, came the next exciting movie scene with a new lead character. The catalyst was again a man, only this time a most unlikely man, especially given the life I was living. I won't give the details of how the event came about, because it would reveal too much. Suffice it to say that one piece was fitting into the next, as always. I had been told, ordered really, by my husband, that I was to be in a particular city for a dinner. I've never been very good with orders, plus on top of this demand for my appearance, I had a strong feeling he was having an affair and I was furious. Of course he denied it, but my intuition was smack on, as it is for most women whose husbands are having affairs. In retaliation, to make him angry, I took a less direct route and flew to another city to spend a couple of days beforehand with friends. I was booked to leave on the Thursday to fly to where I was going for this Friday dinner. Included in my plans was a dinner on Wednesday with someone I really wanted to see—in fact, someone with whom I had entertained the idea of having a love affair when I left the marriage. Life, however, had other plans for me, and on Tuesday I awoke knowing I had to leave on Wednesday rather than Thursday. Although my friends all expressed disappointment at my early departure, and I would have definitely preferred the Wednesday night dinner with my male friend, there was no question for me. I simply knew I had to leave on Wednesday.

During those days, I had access to many services, and even though it was an over-booked flight, I received a seat in the first-class section. (This is going back a long time, way before any of the regulations we now see in place.) When I knew Tuesday morning that I had to leave the next day, I could excitedly feel I was going to meet someone. So it was with a considerable degree of anticipation that I asked the agent at the airport who the first-class passengers were, and although I knew a few of them, none rang the bell for me. Still, there was a nagging feeling in me as I wandered the airport checking out faces. I went into the lounges, as well, but again no bell. Then my attitude shifted to an: "Oh, well," and I basically forgot about it.

When I got onboard, the seat next to me was still unoccupied, though the agent had told me who would be taking it. Well, at least I thought I knew. Instead, about to sit down, was a disheveled mad scientist-type looking character. My criticizing eye scanned him, noting his scruffy worn shoes in need of a polish, his unfashionable pants unlike what a first class passenger *ought* to be wearing, an obviously good cashmere sweater with several equally obvious moth-like holes in it, while his grey hair tied in a non-corporate ponytail set the stage for his eyes framed in old John Lennon style glasses. The unlit pipe dangling from his mouth defined the faint lingering sweet pipe smell. In my then entitled arrogance, I instantly concluded he did not belong in first class, so in my now-British accent I explained he must be in the wrong seat, as he was not who was to sit there. He smiled and simply said: "Oh, we changed seats." As I was having none of this scraggly character, I put the newspaper in front of my face in a self-important manner to avoid any possibility of conversation, and I kept it there through takeoff. A strange thing happened, though. I found, quite literally, that I could not read the words. It was the oddest thing, but that's what was happening. As we became airborne, I finally put down the newspaper, looked at him and said, "Okay, so who are you?" In a throaty humorous tone, he responded with "You're very good. You took a while." That was the beginning of one of the most interesting conversations of my life, along with the beginning of the next scene of my life-movie, even though I certainly wasn't thinking that at the time.

I have referred to this man often as the "Dark Shaman," because he turned my world upside down and taught me more in a short period of time than ten years of workshops ever could have done.

Meanwhile, back at the ranch, the holiday season came and went; guests departed and my children returned to university and to work. Now I could announce to my husband that I was leaving the marriage. Although I felt I had received inner clarity on how I was going to handle the situation, I remember feeling very nervous nevertheless. What if I was wrong in what I was going to propose? I could be left literally destitute, without a career. What if I hadn't heard my message as clearly as I thought I had? My husband was a powerful man with connections. He was also a part of the "old boys' club" that you get into only through the appropriate channels. To go up against this, to receive a settlement, would have taken years of legal fighting, and it was clear that this was not a masculine arena I wanted to enter. Instead, I gave him my two options, neither of which I knew he would want, although one was far better for him than the other. What he couldn't know is that I was playing Russian roulette, because only one option would work for me. In the end, he gave in to what he perceived as being the most advantageous option for him and which, thanks to my guidance, was the only viable one for me. He would now be deprived of the fight and the opportunity to win, and nothing hurts the ego of a powerful man more.

Remember the message that I was to prepare myself and buy a house? I had listened, and because of that I was now able to walk away without being a pawn in the fight of old-boys'-club-powerful-lawyers-pitted-against-powerful-lawyers game in which I would most probably lose. I wasn't going to fight for all the hidden bank accounts and assets I knew were there. I left him with everything he had, untouched. There was no settlement for me other than the profit, minus mortgage payout, on the house that I had remodeled, and greatly contributed to financially, plus that half of the down payment my husband had made on the purchase. I walked away without a battle over money or a weighing of the value of the possessions that I didn't want anyway.

Through this relationship, I was exposed to and expanded by opportunities that belong to only a few. These opportunities have all participated in bringing me to where I am now. The hook, and believe me it was a big hook, was in my giving up all that I had in my life, the ease of daily life, the financial freedom, the excitement, and the exposure to people and events. Through the pain of this marriage, I grew internally. The resistance I had for so long, the resistance to heeding my soul's calling to make self-exploration my priority in life, was the source of the pain. Now my soul had won over my ego. I have neither regrets nor resentments over this marriage. On the contrary, I am grateful for these experiences and I thank this man.

Holding on to any aspect of our lives, regardless of what the unfinished business might be, is one of the biggest drains on our energy. For a long time I *did* blame my husband. I felt it was entirely his fault that I was so unhappy and that the relationship was causing my suffering. Only after years of getting to know myself was I able to see the gifts that had brought me to the place where I could be exceedingly grateful to him for serving as such a powerful catalyst for my own soul journey. I continue to thank him. This was also probably the first time I really understood that *life* doesn't care whether you like the unfolding or not.

At this moment in my writing, I am aware of how I am feeling very exposed, having just shared details with you that few people know. Yet this was a powerful period of my life, a major turning point during which I began to fine-tune myself. As the whole point of this book is to use my stories to show how life has, indeed, magically unfolded for me in spite of me, moving me forward to the next step, I'm willing to feel my own vulnerability. Speaking from my own experience, part of the game of Life seems to be that if we can trust what is in front of us, sincerely knowing we are not in charge, instead of trying to outmaneuver it by being caught in the "wanting to know," we will somehow be taken care of. Of course we often go kicking and screaming to the next scene of our movie, loudly protesting how this is not the way we want it. Although it usually is not apparent at the time, when we honestly look back, the gift becomes obvious.

CHAPTER FIVE:

The Dark Shaman, the Priest-Shaman, and the Heart Shaman

I do not at all understand the Mystery of Grace—only that it meets us where we are but does not leave us where it found us.

Anne Lamott

As I mentioned in the previous chapter, the man I met on the plane would end up turning me and my world upside down in a way that I couldn't possibly have foreseen or "invited" at the time. Certainly, I couldn't have even imagined such a character appearing in my life-script. He was indeed a "Dark Shaman" who showed me a world as different from my own as the two poles of our planet and who taught me more than I could possibly describe. He was a definitive catalyst in my alchemy.

Later I would study Shamanism, and although my friend wouldn't qualify to be called a Shaman in the classic sense, it is nevertheless my descriptive term for him. As I was about to write this chapter, I looked up the word "shaman" in several dictionaries. Of interest to me was that the word "magic," or a reference to magic, was used in all of the definitions. And my friend did introduce me to some magic, for sure!

Shamans are often known for shape-shifting, and he was indeed a shape-shifter. He was a totally elusive person who would appear and disappear so that no one, even those close to him, ever knew his whereabouts unless he appeared in front of you or you knew where he was going. He and I would go for weeks without speaking in person, yet we spoke often in what he referred to as the "inner plane." This was something very new for me, yet it seemed perfectly natural. In the future, I would have many situations to "test" this out and to see the accuracy of our inner-plane communications.

Some of you may have read about someone bi-locating, which means that a person is being seen in one place and at the same time seen in an entirely differ-ent country, for example. That was the case for my friend.

Our communications on the inner plane were very real, although not as clear in detail as a phone conversation would be; nevertheless, the necessary informa-tion was there. Let me tell you of one experience and you can decide. My Dark-Shaman friend and I hadn't spoken on the phone for close to three months. People were calling me from various parts of the world, pleadingly asking if I knew where he was, desperate to try and find him. I felt he was in China and said that to a couple of people. In the meantime, a close girlfriend and I were putting together a trip into the Amazon with a group of people. Besides ourselves, there were several others helping with the logistics and the driving routes to reach our final destination where we would be camping. This was all before the days of personal computers, email, cell phones, texting, or any other rapid form of com-munication ruling our day other than the telephone. Two people called, neither of whom I knew—nor did they know each other—asking to be included on the trip. Although each gave a reasonably obscure, out there explanation of how they had heard about the trip, neither person meant anything to me at the time. Nevertheless, they were both keen to be included, which they were.

Prior to our leaving for the trip, I had told a friend that my Dark-Shaman friend would be meeting us in the jungle, coming there from Chile. He looked at me as though I were crazy, asking in a somewhat snarky tone, "And just how would you know that if you haven't spoken to him for so long?" My girlfriend with whom I was organizing the trip, on the other hand, shares the same wavelengths much of the time, so she didn't doubt my comment.

After four days of serious driving, we arrived at a very small town that would be our last stop before reaching our destination, which was really just a plot of land near to where some friends of friends lived. Our plan was to pick up supplies in town. On entering the first shop, I was greeted with: "Ohhh, you're Beverly! He told us you were coming." The same thing happened in another shop, so it was then clear he would be waiting when we arrived at our destination.

When we got to our camp area, indeed there he was, smoking his pipe, waiting. After our greeting, he asked why we were a day late. Given that there was no way for him to have known any of this, it took me aback until I remembered that we had actually left a day later than originally planned because someone's plane had been delayed, and that made too late a start for that day. When I asked where he had come from, he replied, "Well, you already know—I came up from Chile." And, yes, he had been in China prior to Chile, during the exact time I had said he was.

I mentioned my friend's ability to seemingly bi-locate. This is something that is referred to in Buddhist texts, for example, and certainly in Shamanic ones. There are, in quantum physics and esoteric theories, explanations for how this could occur, which are beyond any attempt on my part to explain. Although I didn't personally experience him being with me at the same time as someone else said he was with them, other people certainly told me, on several occasions, of their experiences.

The day we arrived at our campsite, our group decided we were going to walk down to a place that had been named The Cathedral because those who knew it viewed it as a sacred site. Before leaving the camp, I was telling my friend of our plans. He noticed my brand new, fancy camera that my family had only just given me at Christmas the month before, and looking intensely at me he said, "You're not taking your camera, are you?" "Yes, of course," I said quizzi-cally, meaning without saying, "Why wouldn't I?"

"You are going to a sacred site. Photos should not be taken there." With that, I joined the group and left, thinking "Yeah, whatever. That's really a bit far out for me." I did, however, tell the group what he had said. After our walk in the jungle, down a steep slope, we arrived at a gorgeous waterfall, sitting in sacred silence. The cascade, falling into the magically energized pool of crystalline water, surrounded by the green jungle, dropped everyone into quiet reverence. Our silence, however, quickly turned into excitedly chatting about the beauty of the place while we took pictures, despite the warning. We were then anxious to get into the water. There was nowhere on the ground to leave our cameras, so we put them all in a basket that someone had and placed it on a flat rock at the pond's edge. Just as we were getting into the water, *plop* went the basket into the water. Someone was close by and caught the basket just as it hit the water. My girlfriend and I, who were accustomed to strange and wonderful experi-ences, looked at each other, laughing nervously, as did some others in the group. Having saved the cameras, we now very carefully placed the basket on the flat surface of a rock high above the water. Feeling relieved about the cameras' safety, we all gaily and joyfully jumped in the water to swim to the waterfall. Once we were all out into the lagoon, *plop* went the basket into the deeper water! This time no one was close enough to catch the basket, so all the cameras went to their demise in the sacred pool. Ah, well—nothing to be done now that they were ruined except to retrieve them and to hope that perhaps a picture or two would be had from the adventure.

On returning to the camp, there he was, sitting on the log smoking his pipe. "How was your time at the Cathedral?" he asked, while looking at me with an ever-so-knowing look, adding: "I did tell you that pictures were not to be taken at sacred sites." So he had known what had happened and, indeed, what would happen if we insisted on taking pictures. "Let your mind be your camera and hold the pictures in your awareness," he observed. That was the last camera I ever owned.

Once during devastating floods, I was helping some friends with the massive cleanup of their home. Huge neighborhoods had suffered flooding. In walking the streets to get to my friends' house, I passed home after home with volunteers hauling ruined furniture, other household items, water tanks, furnaces, everything you can imagine out to the closed-off streets. During this experience, I was reminded of my Dark-Shaman friend, with his small canvas bag that contained all of his worldly possessions and his comment about pictures being stored in one's awareness. In contrast, I was struck deeply by things that people want to hang on to in the face of disaster. In one case, I was carefully hand-washing photos, one by one, while someone else was patting them and laying them out to dry. Given the sewer backups plus the flood waters, and if we had been adhering to what the board of health was saying, the photos should all have been thrown out, but the owners wanted them saved. In the midst of their stressful disaster, these had an extreme importance for them. Besides the emotional impact, when people are under such stress, the brain can do something called "switching," a kind of shutting down, and behavior during this time can be quite different from what it might be for a similar situation in different circumstances.

The gift for me in witnessing this saving of pictures was how it caused some personal reflection for me. I was, first, so grateful for having become somewhat of a minimalist in my life, reducing my possessions bit by bit. Yes, of course, there are still lots of "things" in my house that I love. Nevertheless, as time goes by, things themselves have lost their meaning. Although I can still feel some attachment to the beauty of my art works, for example, or a favorite piece of clothing, they really have no value in relationship to my life. I feel I could walk out the door and never come back.

This reflection took me to recalling how my Dark-Shaman friend, with his one small canvas bag, would say to me, "When you can do this, you will know freedom." I knew then, and more so now, that this is absolutely true. My things that I am attached to are a burden to me, and I can feel that burden in my body. My suitcases are getting lighter when I travel—down from two big ones to a medium one and a small one–yet even though I'm working on it, I'm a long way from traveling with one small canvas bag.

So back to the Amazon experience. One evening I decided to sleep out on a hammock rather than in the shelter. Around midnight I woke up to a noise. The camp was located near the base of a hill. From my position in the hammock, I could see light coming from further on, past the hill, and it seemed the noise was also from there. Bear in mind, there were no towns or cities anywhere nearby to cast any kind of light, so whatever could the lights and noise be coming from? Unable to sleep after that, I lay awake and twice observed flashing colored lights in the sky of red, green, and yellow. There was no noise that I could hear associated with these two experiences. Although one airliner did pass overhead during the night, this was not the same as my observation of what I am certain were UFOs. Just before first light broke, while it was still dark, the light from the jungle disappeared and the noise stopped. Although I didn't know it at the time, my girlfriend had also woken up to the same phenomenon, and when we exchanged our stories the next morning, we found they were similar. In case you're wondering, there were no drugs or alcohol of any sort in, or used, in our camp.

When morning arrived I did something pretty stupid from the purely practical point of view. And I still can't believe I actually did this, though, in the same breath, I'm grateful to be alive to tell you the tale. I was so intrigued by the light coming from the jungle, I wanted to explore. One of the guys said he knew the way to the top of the hill and did I want to go? So this is where the stupid part really comes in, because I had only short hiking boots and no sticks to put in front of my steps as we waded through waist-high grass for much of the way. Do you have any idea of what creatures make their way in the tall jungle grasses? Gracias a Dios, it didn't occur to me until much, much later, otherwise I would have probably frozen in fear, fainted, and been a delightful morsel for some of those creatures.

Upon reaching the top of the hill it was immediately obvious why the light had appeared as it had, because there was now, in front of me, a huge vertical drop to the jungle floor. The vast dense jungle appeared never-ending. The vista alone was awe-inspiring, yet the impact of this truly unforgettable sight was in seeing the rain rise from the floor of the jungle—upwards, although there was no moisture at all where we were standing. A soft quiet sound accompanied the misty rain and, as I listened, it was as though I were hearing the Earth breathe. It was at about this time that environmentalists were referring to the jungles as being the "lungs of the Earth," and now I knew why. The gentle inhale–exhale felt hypnotically healing.

The green expanse in front of us was formidable. I was to learn later, in another Amazonian experience, how someone unfamiliar with the jungle can, quite literally, be lost in the jungle after venturing only a matter of feet. There was no sign of even a small clearing in the jungle carpet, and there were no known tribes in the area. The mystery remained: what created the noise that rose out of here during the night? I have my perspective and I leave yours to you. Although there is no direct connection to this shamanic friend and my perspective on what created the noise or the light from the jungle, my sense was he was somehow familiar with what was going on.

My Dark-Shaman friend was a great life-gift, and I knew he was in my life for a purpose as a teacher. I remain enormously grateful to the forces of the Universe that arranged our meeting. I have often said that through my experiences with him I was kicked along the spiritual path by several years. Although I had been interested in expanding my understanding of metaphysical phenomena prior to meeting him, he accelerated this through his example for me. I had been living in the fast lane for many years, which had become a numbing place. As I see it, this is why the gas got turned up to where it was unbearable, leaving me no choice but to leave my marriage. Spending time and having these various experiences with my Dark-Shaman friend quickly shook me out of that numb stupor, starting with our very first conversation on the plane. Having our "inner plane" communication awakened my listening more intently to my own inner voice. Through him I began to see that what we think we know from our blinders-on perspective is nothing more than a belief. Then, what had previously been the unusual for me became the natural.

I have rarely mentioned to anyone that I also feel my Dark-Shaman friend was not of this world. He had an incredibly low heart rate, his skin had an odd tone, and he seemed to possess specific information about other realms of existence. I feel it is highly likely that we have beings from other planets in our cosmos living among us and, to me, he felt like that.

When he was in China, I had a dream. Now, I'm not a big dream person in that I rarely write dreams down, and usually they are lost upon waking. When I woke from this one, however, I had a clear image in my mind that I drew throughout the day, even though I could not recall any content of the dream. After another dream that night, the content of which I also cannot recall, I awoke knowing that I needed to have a ring made from the symbol I had been drawing. That day I went with my design to a jeweler, who said without hesitation: "This is something very spiritual." It was quite a spectacular piece in 18 karat gold, in the shape of a circle with a triangle in the center and a stone at each point of the triangle. I loved the ring and wore it all the time on the middle finger of my left hand. Everywhere I went people would comment on it, from grocery-store cashiers to passengers on airplanes. It drew their attention.

When I went to the Amazon, I left the ring at the home of a friend for safekeeping. After I returned from the trip, I met my Dark-Shaman friend for coffee wearing the ring. He was totally taken by the ring and asked if he could look at it. With hesitation I took it off and handed it to him.

"This is mine, you know," he said. "You need to give it to me."

"No," I replied. "This is my ring - give it back to me."

We then became locked in a silent energetic battle. Although his energy was strong and most people did whatever he said, I felt empowered. We stayed in this tug-of-war space, eyes piercing eyes.

"You *will* give it back to me," I repeated.

All he said then was, "You have won."

He got up and left. That was the last time I saw him, and I no longer wanted to be in touch with him. It was after the Amazon trip and this experience in the coffee shop that I put "Dark" in front of "Shaman" when referring to my friend.

Some time later, I could feel the Dark-Shaman energy wanting to communicate, as we had done before. I can't explain it—I can only say that I knew I had to destroy the ring. Not pass it on to someone else, but destroy it. I remember how, on taking it to the same jeweler to melt it down, I felt both sadness at losing a piece I loved and relief at having let it go. To this day, years since this event, I still have an image, albeit faint now, on my finger of the triangle in what looks like dark freckles for the three points.

I have deliberately repeated myself several times thus far in saying how I see one piece in one's life fitting into the next, and I remain in mindful awareness of that as I am about to tell you of this next experience. It is from a continuous place of awe that I see how all the significant players and events in my life-movie (as in yours) play their role in leading me into the next chapter.

One of the people who had mysteriously called, asking to be included on the trip to the Amazon, introduced me to the person who would now act in this next scene of my movie, and again, who would have quite an impact on my life.

Amusingly, he was also a Shaman, this time following a more accurate definition. He had a fascinating history, starting his adult life as a priest in the High Anglican church. The Church was his life. He had no conscious interest in anything outside of it and certainly not in Shamanism. Yet when Life wants to come through someone in a particular way, the stage gets set. In this case, the priest began saying things from the pulpit, unplanned things that spontaneously came out of him, that were certainly not part of the traditional teachings. Nevertheless, what he said appeared to have great appeal to his parishioners, because the crowds began ballooning whenever he gave a sermon.

During this time, a parishioner was hospitalized with a terminal illness. The family called, asking him to please administer the last sacraments. Those who were present in the room later commented on how, when the priest arrived and was standing in the doorway of the room, there seemed to be a light around him. The priest said he was feeling something very foreign to him, outside his experience. When he got to the bedside of the dying woman, he said to her, "I am going to do something I have never done before and I want to ask your permission," to which she replied, "Yes." His hands went to various parts of her body, pausing over certain areas. Less than two days later, the woman was well enough to leave the hospital, and was still in great health when he last heard of her, several years later.

Although all this happened during the beginning of what was being called "The New Age," the priest, as yet, had no interest in it, nor had he read any of the books that were coming out. He continued giving sermons, and whatever he planned to say turned into what needed to be said instead and simply came through him. By then, the church parking lot, with large loudspeakers, was holding the overflow of people who had come to hear these new concepts.

Eventually the church authorities stepped in with an ultimatum, given that their previous warnings to adhere to their teachings appeared to have gone unheard: "Either preach the word as you have been taught or you must leave the Church."

As soon as he left the church, my friend's archetypal Shaman came forward. An archetype is an energy pattern that transcends all religious and cultural lines. A person cannot be an archetype. Thus, although Joan of Arc is viewed as having been a martyr in her culture and in Catholicism, she herself is not an archetype. As other cultures and religions would not view her as a martyr, she does not transcend the religious and cultural boundaries. "The Martyr," on the other hand, is an archetype.

In my own experience, there was no question for me that energetically this man carried "The Priest" in his blueprint. You would see him and energetically see "The Priest." As an archetype dictates, and most specifically in this case, Life unfolded in such a way that he had had no choice but to become The Priest. The forces of Life will compel the action, and when an archetype expresses that action, the energy will come through, whether you like it or not. Although some people see "The Shaman" and "The Priest" as being quite different from an archetypal and energetic perspective, for me the transition he made from "The Priest" into "The Shaman" seemed nothing more than a different coat on the same energy. In his case, priestly shaman energy had taken over from "The Priest." Shamanic information began to flow through him, and his life experiences supported the information. Instead of speaking from written religious material, he spoke from his experiences and worked with people using Shamanic tools he received among the information.

I lived with this man for a little while, and during this time I went home for a quick visit with my family. While there, I felt drawn to call my cousin, with whom I hadn't spoken for quite some time. It wasn't that we didn't like each other; it was more that we didn't have a lot in common and our lives were very different. My cousin seemed particularly happy to hear from me, and in our conversation she told me how significant it had been to receive a book I had bought for her quite some time before. Her life story included, at the end of her teens, going into a convent to be a nun, although she definitely did not carry the archetype of "The Nun." The book I had given her is one which has remained, through all my house moves, on my bedside table and which, to this day still, many years after first reading it, gives me the same rush of energy whenever I open it and read the first sentence. Here now was my cousin, telling me how this non-religious spiritual book had impacted her and brought her to a place of feeling inner peace, which I could clearly hear in her as she spoke.

I had been back at the Priest–Shaman's place only a short time when, early one morning, I awoke from a disturbing dream. He woke up also, asking me what was the matter, to which I replied: "Someone has died." He was quiet for a minute and then said he would be right back. When he returned shortly, he said that one of the swans living in the large pond at the back of his house had died. It was the female. Swans mate for life, and the male was there by her side, mourning her passing. Then the Priest–Shaman added, "I believe a woman has also died." Within a couple of hours, still in the early morning, the phone rang. It was my mother calling to tell me that my cousin had died suddenly in her sleep, at age fifty.

During our time together, the Priest–Shaman was conducting a vision quest in the Grand Tetons of Yellowstone Park. Much of his work with students was in showing, through his experiences, the connection we can have to animals as part of our connection to all that is. One of the sweetest events of my life happened during this trip—one I am very well aware may stretch my credibility with you to your breaking point. We were each spending a considerable amount of time in silence, and I had gone for a walk by myself. I was in a contemplative space, walking slowly, enjoying the wild flowers, which can be spectacular in this region. In front of me a field mouse stopped and looked up at me with a clump of flowers, like a bouquet, held in its mouth. I can recall how there was only and completely this moment of connection between us, out of time and space. After this moment of looking at me, the mouse dropped the bouquet on the path in front of me and left.

The group spent a couple of days in preparation before hiking up to camp near the base of Mount St. John. The energy of the Teton mountain range is powerful, becoming even more palpable once you have climbed up into quieter space. During one of our group gatherings, following a meditation, several people conveyed how during it, they had seen the two of us (my friend and I) in past native-American times, in specific situations. As each vision was told, I remember seeing the image myself, with great clarity and a sense of truth. There was no question in me that this had been a part of our strong connection.

We could sense a storm coming and quickly packed up the camp, although the sky was still cloudless. My friend and I were making our way across the flat area at the base of Mount St. John, and before we could head down the descent trail, the storm hit with pounding rain, thunder, and lightning. The group was ahead of us and, without speaking, we each started to slow our pace. Then something unfolded that I can only describe as pure magic. Although the storm had not abated at all, there was a spiritual calm, an electrifying energy from the earth and trees and rain, and a sense of being surrounded by ethereal spirits. It was another treasured experience in my life.

Even though our intimate relationship ended, the Priest–Shaman and I remained friends and stayed in touch. It had been quite a number of months since I had heard from him when he called. He wanted to share with me his recent experience of a severe heart attack and surgery. During his open-heart surgery, he had had a near-death experience. He left his body and could view everything that was happening in the operating theatre. Moving "forward" out of the theatre and going to the light, he told how he had met "me." "Go back," I had said, "this is not your time; you still have much work to do." This, according to him, was when he came back into his body. Later, in discussion with the surgeon, he received verification that the team thought they had lost him, then he had come back to life. That was not his time.

As I was writing this section, my Priest–Shaman friend died suddenly. It was a few days before I heard of his passing, at which time I sat for a meditation. In my mind, just as I started my mediation and even though he had already been gone for a few days, I told him to go with the light. I heard him laughing his special laugh and saying, "The light is always there and it's instant!" With a pang of remembrance, just for a moment, I once again felt his large energetic healing hands on me as though it were happening in person.

Our minds automatically want to search for an explanation—a useless task—when unusual phenomena occur. Underlying this need to know about that which cannot be explained lies the overwhelming bigness of life and our connection to all that is.

It is still with awe that I recall how it was that I found my way to my main teacher, Brugh Joy. I call him "The Heart Shaman" here because of an experience near the end of his life, which he spoke of. He was in Tibet visiting one of the high mountain villages that was a sacred Buddhist site. As he entered the village, an old woman came over to him, put her hand on his heart and welcomed him, calling him "The Heart Shaman." Indeed, although unknown to her, he would tell students how "The Heart Center unites all things and it breaks up any kind of belief system that tends to be too small for the soul."

I heard of Brugh through my closest friend and ally on my sacred journey. She sent me Brugh's first book, *Joy's Way*, and as soon as I read it I called to see about getting into a class. That was December and the next foundational class was starting at the end of that month. Alas, it had been full for some time and there was a long waiting list. Nevertheless, I was told that the organizers would call if a space became available. A mere couple of days before Christmas I received a phone call saying there had been a cancellation and the spot was mine if I wanted to come. I was to learn only much later that when a space opened up, Brugh himself would go down the waiting list and determine the order of those who would be asked to fill the spot. Although I had to make considerable adjustments to make it to this class, including switching family plans so that I could leave on Christmas Day to drive for four and a half days, there was no hesitation.

The night before I was to arrive at the lodge, I had a dream in which a wolf spoke to me. I couldn't remember the details, yet I still remember how it felt special to me that morning. As I was nearing the lodge, driving through desert terrain of rolling sage brush and short plants, it *just so happened* that I looked up to the top of a hill I was passing to see a wolf standing there looking down at me. I felt I was being welcomed to Brugh's.

What an incredible gift Brugh was in my life! He was considered the master of shadow material and could take a willing participant deep into their internal caverns. Our beliefs, the large majority of which are elusive and hidden in our unconscious—the shadow—ironically are the underbelly that dictates our life show. It is the unclaimed pieces of ourselves that determine how we respond or react to life. (Going even further into the dark with a master such as Brugh taps into the Transcendent, although this is not a subject to be dealt with here.)

I remember so well a particular day when, sitting opposite my teacher during one of my earlier classes with him, his piercing blue eyes pinning me down across the circle, he said: "You are your mother!" I gasped, choked, and ran from the room to vomit. Do you think maybe I had a reaction to what he had said?!

It's amusing to me now to remember my reaction, yet at that time in my life it was horrifying to me that I was in any sense my mother. My understanding of the profundity of his statement completely eluded me, and from this place of extreme defense, I took it all personally. It would be many years before

I reached a place of deep compassion for my mother, of seeing her beauty as a perfect human being who lived her life doing the best she could, and, most importantly, of coming to the depth of understanding that yes, I am my mother as you are yours.

At that time, however, I was stunned. Surely, my teacher could see that I was the exact opposite of my mother. Couldn't he see that I had been doing everything to not be my mother? Little did I know at the time, but my denying my mother and trying so desperately to not be like her was exactly the resistance I needed to face.

My mother's greatest gift to me was in being my biggest trigger. I was gifted with opportunity after opportunity to witness my reactions to her, each one internally chipping away a tiny piece of my resistance. And it was from my resistance to being like my mother that I came to live my life very differently. If we look at family patterns, we are able to see how there are un-canny similarities in the way various members of the family respond to life. My mother was driven by fear and lack, whereas my motto from as early in life as I can remember was like the book title: "Feel the Fear and Do It Anyway." One of the most painful pieces of my earlier experience of my mother, and actually one that went on well into my adulthood, was when she would say, "Why can't you be like everyone else?" To me that was tantamount to suicide. Why ever would I want to be like everyone else?! Yet embedded in my attitude was a piece of "specialness" to protect against feeling "ordinary." And so it was that I had to find the ordinary pieces of myself. In taking on both poles, and in becoming friendly with those less savory, didn't-want-to-have pieces of myself, as well as those that I found "desirable" about myself, I slowly realized that everything my mother was, I was also.

From the collective perspective, we each hold the potential of all that is. For example, we each carry the potential of being a Hitler or a Saddam Hussein. That does not mean it is in our life story to be either of these men, but it does mean acknowledging the potential. So it was then, in the eventual stripping away of the resistance, of owning all of my mother within me, that I was opened to the compassion of seeing my mother's full humanness. In doing so, I also became compassionate with myself and my own humanness.

There were many times, though, when I literally felt that I would not survive Brugh and my exposure to my dark pieces. It all felt way too big for me then, but I have since thanked the Universe many times and will continue to do so for having put Brugh in my life script. Doing his foundational intensive was a definitive turning point in my life, started by my dear friend and her gift of Brugh's book. I continued working with Brugh as my teacher for many years.

I see the above events and all the others throughout this book as beautiful, magical stories, none of which I could have created. To try, even for a moment, to explain the magic would be of no value and serve only to diminish the richness of the experience.

CHAPTER SIX:

Where Did this "Me" Start? ...or, the beginning of beliefs

You believe in free will.

You believe you make yourself sick.

You believe you choose your parents.

You believe you can control your dreams.

You believe you can take charge of your life.

You believe you have the power of prayer.

You believe you can make a difference.

You believe your pain is your fault.

You believe you can do better.

You believe you are responsible.

You believe all sorts of shit.

Ram Tzu knows this:

When God wants you to do something

You believe it is your idea.

Ram Tzu aka Wayne Liquorman

In order to begin this exploration, we have to examine just where all of our life-rules have come from. Why is it that we are the way we are? Although this might seem tedious, understanding the beginning of beliefs and how they turn into our conditioned reactions to life is critical to the examination of those beliefs.

In order to look at the beliefs we hold so dear, it is important to first understand the difference between *response* and *reaction*. *Responding* to some aspect of life is like receiving. We experience something, have a feeling about it perhaps or act on it in some way, and then along comes the next experience. There is no charge, no holding on to the experience. *Reaction*, on the other hand, is very different because instead of responding, one or more of our *buttons* have been pushed. The button gets pushed because of our strongly held belief(s) related to what has just occurred. I discuss this in greater detail further in this chapter, but for now the way we can distinguish between a button being pushed and a response is that a *button-pushing reaction* will be accompanied by some sort of body clue. This may be, for example, a tightening in the stomach area, or a burning sensation, or a headache, or a kink in the neck, simply a contraction of muscles, or whatever. The point is that the body will give you a signal that a button has been pushed. The reaction we experience when an external event pushes one of our buttons generally includes, along with the body sensation, either finger-pointing blame projected onto someone else, making them the cause of your distress, or denial as a defense against what the external event is evoking. There is an energetic charge that will stay in the body until what is under the reaction is released. We'll see later where these reactions are coming from.

I have been a teacher of change for many years. One of the BodyTalk courses I taught during this time dealt with the early formation of belief systems, how they turn into our responses or conditioned reactions to life, and thus how they impact every aspect of our lives. It was through teaching this class that I discovered where I like to hang out because, indeed, where we are living our lives from, how we interact with others, and how life is or is not working for us comes from these early imprints of belief systems. From these early imprints, we formulate our concepts of who we believe ourselves to be. We begin to identify with "Me."

What makes you feel heavy? What makes you feel light? Try this simple little test of checking in with yourself: Are you feeling heavy or are you feeling light? Later we'll see how this also is a good check for whether or not you are in your truth. Or if you have a charge around someone or something in your life at the moment, think of it now and check in with yourself: Are you feeling heavy or are you feeling light?

So where do these beliefs about ourselves come from? And who are "We"? In order to answer this, we need to go back to the time of our conception, when the sperm hit the egg. I imagine we are all aware that half of our genetic material comes from our father and half from our mother. My mother had in her gene pool half from her father and half from her mother, just as my father did from his parents, and so on. That's the basic biology and is true for all humans.

You may wonder how imprinting could begin as early as the fetal stage of life, yet there is a great deal of scientific evidence available today regarding the impact of events on a fetus. For example, a pregnant woman can be, let's say, in San Francisco while her child's father is in New York City. In other words, there is physical separation. Electrodes to register the fetal activity are placed on the woman's abdomen. When the father is placed under high stress, this is registered immediately as stress on the fetus, which is thousands of physical miles away. The Russians did a similar experiment with baby rabbits, which were taken on a submarine into the Black Sea, and the submarine submerged to a considerable depth. Shock was applied to the babies and immediately the mother, who had been wired with electrodes and left on shore, registered panic and physical stress. While these and other similar experiments bring home the obvious relationships between child and parent, and the impact of external events, what is important is the illustration that physical presence is not necessary for an energetic connection. In quantum physics terms, we are energetic beings made of particles of energy. Communication and connection are energetically instant, and actual physicality is not required. When a person has an experience of spaciousness in which there is no body and there is no "I," it is even questionable whether we are even particles of energy. We see that this physical existence, which we give so much significance to, has nothing whatso-ever to do with who we *truly* are.

Each experience of a fetus, followed by each experience in the first seven years of that child's life, forms the beginning of the webs of beliefs, which then become the person's self-identification, the false "Me," the personality, along with their responses and now-conditioned reactions to life. The beliefs become the filters, the colored glasses through which we experience everyone and everything.

In a session I was doing with a client, it came up that there had been some trauma when her mother had been three months pregnant with her. When I relayed this information to my client, she responded by saying that she had been told how her father had pushed her mother down the stairs when she was three months pregnant, in an effort to cause a miscarriage. In my own case, when I was looking at this a few years back, it was painful to recall my own mother's story around her pregnancy with me. My brother was nine years older than myself, and my parents were definitely not the perfect couple. My mother, often with bitterness, had told me the story several times of how my father "had taken advantage of her and she got pregnant" with my brother, implying she wouldn't have married him otherwise. My mother, a very capable woman and certainly one with the character of a survivor, told me how she had been planning to leave my father, then she got pregnant with me. In her eyes, I had cost her freedom. Each of these experiences, although very different in the story, may perhaps have the common thread of an unconscious feeling of not being wanted.

I imagine it is not difficult for you to see how these experiments and experiences, although dissimilar, illustrate the beginning of our beliefs. Let's put it in a more graphic way. Imagine a baby being born in a warm, cozy environment, with dimmed lights and Mozart or Beethoven playing in the background. The loving and attentive father is there with the mother, nurturing, offering his support and awaiting the birth of *their* child. When the child is born, what will be the first imprints from its first life experiences? Contrast this with a child born in a speeding ambulance, siren blaring, the mother fighting for her life following a car accident in which the father was killed. What do you imagine will be this child's first imprints?

Basically, we experience life through our senses of smell, taste, hearing, seeing, and touch. (Although it is true that there is a sixth sense and more, I am referring here to the basic senses through which we all experience the world around us.) It seems as though whenever we have an experience, the memory attaches itself, as it were, to a similar type of previous experience. To see that more visually, imagine a sticky spider's web. Spider webs are really fascinating, so allow me a slight digression for a minute. Did you know that the spider spins one string that is not sticky and then the next string that is sticky? What happens then, for example, is that a fly will get caught on a sticky string, hence its inability to get away, while the spider runs up and down the non-sticky string to where the fly is, enabling the spider to eat the fly or preserve it with a web, without a fight or flight from the fly.

Now imagine the building of beliefs as being like the first fly stuck on a sticky string of a spider web. Other flies, when they see the fly that's stuck, might go to the rescue and they get stuck also. Over time there's a huge pile of flies on one string and a huge pile of perhaps ants on another, and so on. In life terms, let's say the newborn child is in intensive care. Generally this will mean the child is in an incubator, unclothed, electrodes on their little body, and maybe even a tube down the throat. The child is also likely to have blood taken, perhaps the jab of needles to set up an intravenous feed or injections for some reason. What will be the experiences, through the five senses, that this child will have? "Touch hurts" will be a likely one. The exposed little body with only a diaper or perhaps not even that, drinking from a bottle held by the nurse through the rubber hole on the side of the incubator, will translate differently than warm, loving cuddling by the mother and the smell of her sweet breast milk.

Thus begins the early imprinting. I'll continue with the example of "touch hurts." If there are further instances, perhaps a slap from a "loving parent" or more serious physical abuse of some sort, the imprinting begins to build into a conditioned reaction to life that the person will have in relationship to touch. Touch is not comfortable, touch is not loving, touch betrays love—these might be some of the ways in which these beliefs could shape up. Similar memories, like flies, add to the conditioning while the belief burrows deeper, out of our sphere of conscious awareness. During the first impressionable seven years, any experiences related to touch or intimacy in this case will set the stage for the continual layering of beliefs related to these initial experiences.

If we grow up in a home where there is physical abuse, let's say, this imprinting can develop into an unconscious belief such as: "I deserve abuse because I'm bad," which can then play out in many different ways in that person's life. Anyone working in this area of abuse knows that the feeling of "deserving to be abused" is a common scenario with clients and often a key, albeit unconscious, piece that can keep the abused person in the abusive relationship. Hearing parents fighting over money, or growing up in poverty without basic life comforts, can manifest later perhaps into never feeling as though there is enough, regardless of how much money one earns. Very often extremely wealthy people cannot really truly enjoy their money because today is not yet the day when there will be enough. (John Paul Getty, one of the wealthiest men in the world at the time, when asked, "When will you have enough money?" responded with "Not today.") Or perhaps the opposite could be that money is evil, it creates fighting and unhappiness, so it manifests in the person being unsuccessful in earning or keeping money. You can see this with people who have the ability to earn lots of money but then immediately lose it, and then they earn it again and lose it again. This is a cycle that might be speaking to this concept, or perhaps to "I'm not worthy of having the money," or a combination of various similar imprints. Although certain themes can be seen often, illustrated through the use of these simple examples, we must remember the uniqueness of each individual. Two children raised in the same home with the same parents will very likely have entirely different concepts running their unconscious behavior. For example, a friend was telling me of a conversation with her sister about a particular family event in which my friend humorously asked, "Are you *sure* we're from the same family?"

It's likely that you have had a similar experience of being around a newborn, as in the following example. The grandparents, both sets, have come to see this new little person, the special carrier of *their* genes. The parents, like most parents, of course think their child is *the* most beautiful and most awake baby ever born, while the grandparents are very likely doing the proud grandparent bit, gushing over every excruciatingly minor detail to their friends. So here's this little baby, lying in the crib, with four gigantic heads (adult heads are gigantic when draped over the railing and you're this tiny person!) of the grandparents, two on each side, gawking and cooing while the parents wait for their child to be praised. The baby now smiles at one of the cooing adults peering at it, and everyone goes crazy with glee. "Oh my gosh, what an adorable baby!" or perhaps: "Did you see, did you see how he smiled at *me*?" The parents are beyond thrilled that their child has appropriately greeted the grandparents. The baby is now intrigued. "Wow, that was cool. I made everyone go nuts with excitement, so let me try that again," and the baby once again offers a smile, only this time bigger. This time he gets even more attention than from the first smile. His internal message is: "Hey, I think I've got this. If I smile, I get lots of attention!"

What happens, then, when the baby starts crying and won't stop? Frustration sets in for the parents. Underneath it all, they feel inadequate because they can't get their child to stop crying. If it's one of the grandparents, perhaps it might be more like: "Oh my. Maybe she doesn't like me." Around and around it goes; the child cries, gets the attention, and cries some more. Imprinting on: "Be good and smile," and "If I cry, I get lots of attention," has begun, and the child is only a newborn.

The critical parent may not consciously or intentionally criticize the child or see what they say as criticism, even when it is pointed out. For the child, pleasing the critical parent can translate out to a way of being in the world as the child develops. Grades in school and achievement are a good example. The child energetically picks up on the disapproval of the parent for grades and achievement perceived as low. The parent is more than likely unaware that the reason they are harboring this sentiment is because they do not want to be seen as having failed in making their child smart. And worse, if their child doesn't learn how important excelling grades are, how in the world will their special child ever get into the proper university? Whew! Isn't it easy to see how out of this kind of scenario augmented by similar experiences, the child develops an unconscious sense of lack of worth, of never being able to get it right. "I can never satisfy you," or "No matter what I do, it is never good enough," or simply "I'm not good enough." On an energetic level, the child has learned that certain kinds of behavior are acceptable while others are not. Although no one experience on its own will create the belief, each criticism gets registered and becomes a fly on the sticky paper. Trying to make a child stand or walk early might be another example. And having children identify words before being able to crawl seems to be an indicator that parents seek these days. The list really is endless, and the purpose here is only to illustrate how one experience adds to another. By the time there are enough flies for what is acceptable, performance anxiety can also begin to form.

A word of caution: I'm using these simple examples as illustrations only. None of these can be called the root cause of anything, nor can any single experience be separated out from other experiences. Rather, I have used them simply to show how, from that first fly, the stickiness builds, one event layering on top of another, into a conditioned reaction to a particular aspect of life.

I'd like to explain how I see this. We are all humans and live human lives. No one is to blame; this is *absolutely not* about blame nor the *poor-me* place. My mother and father did their best, whatever was in front of them, just as your parents did. As an aside, and with a degree of amusement at myself, I want to share with you how I have had many moments in which I have felt so sorry for myself, lamenting what a terrible mother I have been. Usually, of course, I did this with my children. When I would start on this sorry bit, they delighted in turning the screws by exaggerating all the stories they could think of that had "damaged them" along the way, proving just how bad a mother I had indeed been. In reality, however, from their perspective, they do not consider me a bad mother at all. They were simply reflecting how I was seeing myself in this way.

One of the key and tricky pieces around beliefs is that, generally speaking, most people are not aware of their predominant beliefs simply because these have become the conditioned reactions to life. In this conditioned sense, the beliefs are elusive to us, meaning that we are not consciously aware of their influence. To add to that, the beliefs that we hold most dear, the ones that we absolutely think *are* "right," are the ones most in the way of our own self-understanding. I am only mentioning this here and will elaborate later.

We all use coping tools in our lives. They protect us from what we might not yet be ready to explore. Underlying the explanations, the purpose of the coping tools is to give the illusion of feeling safe. It's when we dig deep, after peeling off all the layers, that our need for safety is found. Our feeling of needing to be in control, our need to know, our questioning of why things are going on—all are nothing more than the seeking of safety.

Now that we have looked at some examples of early imprinting, I hope it will be obvious how beliefs tend to get set in place. To see how beliefs translate out to our life experiences, I'll give you what I consider to be a useful illustration.

There is a wise story in India about a man in the Himalayas who is so envious of the eagle, of its high soaring freedom, that his envy has become an obsession. He keeps trying to catch the golden eagle so he can study him and thus learn from him how to fly.

One day he sees there is a nest and waits patiently until the eagle has gone hunting before climbing to the nest and stealing an egg. He takes the egg home and puts it in his chicken coop with a hen that later hatches the baby golden eagle. "Ahhha," he thinks, "now I am going to be able to study the eagle and thus learn how to fly!"

The baby eagle is born in the chicken coop and grows up as a chicken. He walks like a chicken, talks like a chicken, and most importantly, he thinks like a chicken.

One day he sees a gorgeous, huge golden eagle flying high, high, high in the sky and circling above him. "Oh my, oh my," says the chick-eagle with deep longing, "I so wish I could fly like that." The majestic eagle cries out to the young one, "Come, come little one. Come fly with me. I will teach you how to fly like an eagle for you are an eagle, not a chick."

The young eagle cries back, "But I can't. I can't fly. I'm not supposed to fly. Can't you see I'm only a chick, and chicks can't fly?"

I don't know about you, but this story was so poignant to me and remains that way even now as I pass it on to you. Some of you may be feeling like screaming encouragement to the chick, as I remember I felt, because you know he is an eagle. Why can't he see that for himself? You want him to know who he is! So what is keeping the chick from flying? This wonderful story illustrates perfectly our own self-imposed limitations in life. Indeed, this is how we begin our limited existence rather than flying high and free as the eagle. The initial seeds are set, like the fly or the ant on the sticky spider web. As the pile of belief seeds grows from each experience, we become more and more conditioned by our beliefs.

Yet we are not our beliefs. The *true essence* of who we are is beyond beliefs and physicality. Like the baby eagle's yearning to live his true nature and fly, we, too, have a deep yearning to return to essence. The newborn infant does not feel separate from the mother. There is only Oneness. "Me" and "You" doesn't exist yet because there are not enough experiences to form the beliefs that lead to the false identification of "Me" and "You." It is the initial experiences followed by similar experiences that form our beliefs and thus our self-imposed chains of limitations.

A meaningful piece I read in one of Dan Millman's books has stayed with me for years. A couple living in Hawaii have a son aged two or three. Then they have a girl. The boy keeps pestering his parents because he wants to go into the bedroom to talk to his baby sister on his own, with the door to the room closed. The parents resist for fear he wants to cause her harm from jealousy, yet the boy is persistent. Finally, they agree. Watching through the keyhole of the closed door, they see the little boy go to his sister's crib and then say to her, "Please tell me about God before you forget." It was one of the most powerful lines I've ever encountered and has me teary-eyed just recalling it.

It is said that a newborn has the same consciousness as a person of 85 years of age; in other words, age has nothing to do with consciousness. In the above story, the infant girl is still in the space of Oneness. Even though the initial beliefs are beginning to form, for her there is no separation yet. It is only once the experiences build, forming the initial filters, that the memory of being one with all-that-is begins to be forgotten.

Beliefs are concepts, and all concepts are false. This becomes self-evident when we examine beliefs. In the case of the chick that is really an eagle, he nevertheless has the belief that he is only a chick. So although the belief is false, and being a chick is not his true nature, he is convinced he is a chick and he therefore cannot fly. His mother raised him with this belief, taught him how a chick is supposed to behave, and he lives in the chick "culture" with peer pressure from the other chicks. This story, in addition to the couple of examples I gave earlier, illustrates how our initial experiences in life become a stickiness on which energetically similar experiences land. The more similar experiences we have that drop on this sticky string, the stronger the imprint becomes for that belief. The stronger the particular imprint, the more energetically it rests in our body like a dense chunk of cement.

Let's go back to my statement that all beliefs are false. If you look at your own beliefs, where do they come from? This is astonishingly simple, yet so many people never ask the question. You learned your beliefs from others, while they, in turn, learned their beliefs from others—and further back it goes. Yet these beliefs have nothing to do with your own internal truth.

Of course, the point is that most of our beliefs are conditioned, meaning that we are unconscious of them. Think of this as being like when you're driving a route you take every day to work. The trip has become rote memory; there is no thought or thinking required. It is the same with our conditioned reactions. They are deeply embedded in us and dictate how we live, even though we are totally unaware of them. We react to situations and people from these beliefs that actually have nothing to do with what is currently happening. The good old example of the cap off the toothpaste illustrates this. Does the person start screaming at the person who left the cap off *because* the cap had been off? No, absolutely not. Let's look at that.

We've just established how our beliefs are largely unconscious. Even by our teens, there are already layers and layers of experiences, plus the morphing of these layers, which create our beliefs. An *external factor* can be the lid off the toothpaste, a person or an event, or even an article we have been reading in the newspaper or something on the evening news. The external factor is "out there." It is external to you, and it doesn't matter what the external factor itself is. The point is that when we experience an external factor, and when that external factor causes an *internal reaction* in you (remember, reaction is different from response), it indicates that you have been triggered because of some belief you hold as true. One of the more difficult pieces to digest for many people is that when an *external factor* is a *catalyst* for your *internal reaction*, that reaction is never ever about the external factor. The reaction is only ever about you! Let's say your friend or partner or work colleague makes a comment to you, about you. Or better yet, you hear about the comment from someone else. You react by feeling angry or perhaps hurt or maybe unworthy. You might then attempt to defend against the comment, denying its truth. In this case, the external factor has been a person who has just served you, has been a gift to you, by being a catalyst for your internal process in pushing one of your internal buttons. The person has hit on an unconscious piece, an unclaimed and *resisted* piece, within you. The gift is in the invitation to explore what piece in you, related to the comment, that you are resisting.

Now, going back to the toothpaste example, we see the same dynamic. The person's screaming reaction (as opposed to response) has nothing whatsoever to do with the external factor of the cap being off. Rather, the cap being off serves to trigger unconscious, deeply-held-on-to beliefs that had been *building up* until the explosion.

Often, when we are in relationship and unwilling to be in our truth (or unaware of what that means), we will suppress what is really going on for us.

For example, someone asks you if you like what they're wearing and you say you do even when you don't, or you say you agree with a point in a discussion when you don't. These are all lies, albeit small ones. This is what the archetype of "The Prostitute" is about: every time we lie by suppressing our truth we are selling a bit of our soul. If suppression of our truth is a pattern in the relationship, the lid will eventually blow off, as with the over-reaction to the toothpaste cap. Sometimes this reaction may be in a physical form: for example, when we have a heart attack or severe digestive issues.

If you can bear with its length (Indian stories are usually long!), here is another great story from India related to the "where" we react from.

A husband and wife are going to have some friends over for dinner. The wife has a reputation for being a good cook, and she wants her dinner to show this off. She writes a list of groceries for her husband, admonishing him that he must get absolutely every ingredient, as each is significant in her planned dishes. At the little store, he carefully checks the list and leaves feeling satisfied he has correctly done what she told him to do. He walks home along the country dirt road.

Meanwhile in the city, there is an aggressive young man who is intent on climbing the corporate ladder. He has set himself the goal of being promoted to the next higher position. He is so certain he is going to receive this promotion that he rewards himself by buying an expensive, over-his-current-budget sports car. When he is called into the CEO's office, excitedly anticipating the promotion, he is instead told why he was not chosen for the position. Furious, he leaves, gets into his now unaffordable sports car, and drives off in a rage out to the country where he can drive like the crazy man he is at the moment.

Back now to the husband carrying his bags of groceries, walking down the dirt road. The fast sports car comes roaring down the narrow road and brushes against the man, who is now sent tumbling with his groceries. The car doesn't stop, of course. As the man picks himself up, feeling shaken at the realization that he was nearly killed, he notes his torn clothes, some small cuts from the rocks, the groceries strewn all over, and many of the jars now broken. As best he can, he gathers what's left and makes his way home.

When he arrives, his wife begins screaming at him. "How am I now going to cook dinner? My reputation will be ruined. It will be all your fault!" He begins screaming back, "Can't you see I am hurt? You don't even care that I almost got killed trying to get your groceries!" In the doorway, watching in fear, is the couple's four-year old boy. He doesn't like it when his parents fight, which is frequently, so he runs outside to play with his friend on the street. He tells his friend, who replies, "My parents fight like this, too."

Fast forward to when the boys are in their teens, have moved to the city, and have now formed a gang. They get in a fight with another gang, and the boy whose father went for the groceries now kills a young boy from the other gang.

So finally (I *did* tell you it was a long India-style story) we come to ask who is responsible for the boy being killed. Was it the fellow in the rival gang's "fault" he got killed? As with the explosion over the toothpaste cap, the killing of the boy had nothing to do with that moment. What is important to see is how it is not possible to separate out any one reason for why this young man held certain beliefs, built upon since conception, that dictated his particular reaction to the situation, allowing him to take the life of another person. None of us *reacts* just based on what is in front of us; we respond to what is in front of us, but when there is a *reaction* it is *accompanied by a story*. We are each a walking life story. All of our unique experiences, everything about our lives, all the stories we hang on to, dictate how we will interact with what shows up in front of us. We can see how it is not personal, and we can respond less defensively once we understand that we can never possibly know the inner workings of another, of what is happening for them in any given situation. Indeed, the same is true for ourselves.

The story illuminates other pieces, as well, as I imagine you may have noted while you were reading it. The wife, for example, was concerned about what her friends *would think of her* if the meal was not perfect, because she had her identity tied up in her reputation as an amazing cook. The husband, who was going to make sure he did as he had been told, may have felt he had "failed"—perhaps "I can never please her"—and therefore would likely suffer. The guy with the car would have his own life stories around being overlooked for the promotion and his anger at a perceived rejection. And on it goes.

The interesting thing about these imprints that become our conditioned beliefs is their uniqueness. Imagine the following scenario and you may recall a similar one in your own family. There's a family gathering and everyone is sitting around talking about some previous event a few years back. One person says, "Do you remember when Johnny hid the cat in the dryer?" Everyone agrees, with laughter. Someone then says something else about the event and, again, everyone agrees. But now one identical twin makes a comment. Again, everyone agrees, but then the other twin says, "Well, that's true, but you're also forgetting…" The first twin says, "No, no, you've got that wrong." Several others at the table now chime in, each with their own twist on the original comment.

I used identical twins in this example because they would have been born at the same time, then raised in the same family, culture, socio-economic setting, and religion. Nonetheless, they each have their own unique experiences that have colored their perception of life events. As with everyone at the gathering, each person is recalling their own perception of how they viewed a specific event, and while everyone may have a similar recall, there are also differences.

The law used to rely heavily on eyewitness accounts, which convicted many innocent people and sometimes ended in wrongful executions. Once the highly accurate DNA testing came into use, it was shown time after time that the person convicted, based on eyewitness accounts, was in fact innocent and could not possibly have committed the crime for which they had been convicted. Simple eyewitness studies illustrate shocking variations among the witnesses. Staging a car accident, for example, and getting eyewitness accounts from four individuals will repeatedly produce four clearly distinct accounts of how the accident occurred.

So, again, our beliefs become the filters—our own colored glasses—through which we experience everything, giving each of us our unique perception. Although it has become popular to say, "We determine our own reality," what is so often crucially missing is this underlying understanding.

We tend to speak habitually and therefore express many beliefs during the day without giving a thought to them. I often catch myself, for example, saying some conditioned parrot-type phrase, only to then have to say, "That's not what I wanted to say, that's no longer true for me," or something to that effect. The point is that we all utter pat phrases loaded with beliefs every day. We also judge and compare all the time. I'm amused when I hear others say how they try everything not to judge and are then mortified when they still find themselves judging. From my experience and that of others, it seems that just noting a judgment increases our awareness, and thus a shift occurs from judgment itself to a bigger space. Judging ourselves for judging is a resistance to claiming our judge.

Again, the serious introspective question: Where do your beliefs and your reactions to life come from? Who told you that such and such a thing was the truth, the "way it is"? Once you begin to examine this in your life, you will see how you were just told that things are a certain way, period. After you've heard these throughout your childhood—and witnessed certain actions that go along with the beliefs, because other people in your life are operating from the beliefs they've been teaching you—your pile of filters around similar beliefs has grown into a big clump that is now really stuck on a sticky string.

Think of all the various influences you've encountered since you were conceived and in your mother's womb, and how all of them participated in your early imprints and later. These include influences such as your family of origin. What nationality is your family? What is the culture and race of each parent? What was the geographic location of the origins of the family? What is the historical religion of the family and of your upbringing? What about socio-economic status—was your family born or raised in a class-structure society, or part of a wealthy upper class?

It is apparent from a number of studies that we inherit memory. This could be from generations of ancestors or from the collective energy and its influence. In Israel, for example, there are psychiatrists and clinical psychologists who work with young children experiencing nightmares. Many generations after certain events, these children make drawings of buildings or tell stories—based on their nightmares—that give exact details, often including names of people who died in the holocaust. They were not exposed to this information at home or school, and the names they give are not of family members. The buildings they draw appear as they once did. The same thing is happening in Japan where young children, again several generations later, describe in great detail the bombing of Hiroshima. Various forms of therapy acknowledge how these past energies can impact a client.

Another perhaps familiar example is about babies and water. One baby loves the bath, splashing with their hands and feet, squealing with obvious delight, while another screams in terror every time they are bathed, despite being securely held by the parent. Why is one child born with a fear of water and another not? Some people love an open fire, such as outdoors on a camping trip, or following fire trucks to watch devastating fires with awe, while others shrink away from any flame at all.

However we want to look at this, from the genetic perspective as seen in Dr. Candace Pert's work or the morphogenetic fields proposed in Dr. Rupert Sheldrake's work, it is known that we inherit not only our physical traits and characteristics but also collective memory, prejudices, beliefs, and emotions. All is connected. Like many others working in the field of consciousness, I use the analogy of the ocean to illustrate our gene pool and the collective pool of consciousness. In Advaita Vedanta philosophy, the ocean is the sea of consciousness, containing the collective energies of the universe, of all possibilities, and is referred to as the Mahat. Now imagine yourself, your gene pool, and the morphogenetic fields you resonate with as coming from a bucketful of water drawn from the sea. In that bucket will be many fish, sea creatures, and maybe a few sharks—think of these as bits and pieces of unresolved energies from the collective pool of consciousness. Imagine also that your bucket contains many of the same fish, etc. as your parents' buckets did, given that the bucket is being drawn from a similar location in the sea that led to the family traits and memories. Viewed from this perspective, it is not difficult to see the thread of memory, such as the abject fear of water, as being unrelated to this lifetime.

I will say more about the Mahat at another point, but for now I bring it up just to make these analogies, giving us a way to describe the bigger picture, which has nothing to do with the "Me," the little self.

So going back to the conditioning: we become conditioned in our behavior because we have been told repeatedly, in various ways, what is "good" behavior and what is "bad." Yet who actually defines right and wrong? Where did the person who is telling you about something being "wrong" learn that it was so? Have you ever thought about this?

When we are told we are "bad" at an early age, for example, it can have a tremendous impact on us later. Yet who determines what action should be labeled "bad"? Starting at age six, and continuing for six years throughout grade school, I was always getting the strap during Catechism classes. I was viewed as being "disruptive" by the teacher, by my mother, and by the conforming fellow students. The "disruptive," however, was really in reference to not playing by the rules. I was not accepting what I was being told as the truth. I wanted to know more. Had I been referred to by another adjective, such as "precocious" or "inquisitive," how might that have influenced some of the detours I took in my life?

Once our beliefs are fairly set up by age seven, although still to be added to throughout life, we now become involved in various identifications of ourselves. We fall into the illusion that how we appear to the world actually is who we are. These identifications strengthen as they become more embedded in us; for example, the parent with empty nest syndrome or the corporate executive who are heavily invested in these roles. What these people have in common is the *attachment to their role* with which they have become pathologically identified.

The reason the mother experiences an empty nest, which might include physical as well as emotional symptoms, is because her raison d'être—her reason to live, in her mind—has been taken away. Since having children, her focus has been on the sacrificing mother role, giving whatever it takes so that her children turn out the way they are *supposed to*. She could smile sweetly with shy "thank yous" whenever her children were praised because, in her psyche, the praise belonged to her. Now the children are gone, off to university or trekking somewhere. Who is she without the children? Everything she's built into her identification as an attentive mother has suddenly been stripped away and she's left feeling naked. How will people see her? What is life about if not taking care of the family? Often, rather than shifting from this role, the mother in desperation will cling to their child's life, relishing the *life their child has created* and using it to continue to illustrate how "proud" she can be.

Similar, and in most cases more severely felt, is the role of the executive—*the boss*. She or he becomes so identified with the role of being in charge, in control of everything, that forced retirement can be literally a death sentence. You hear all the time about people dying shortly after retirement. "What a shame," people say, "He just retired last year and was really looking forward to golf every day." Although part of that is probably true, that's the conscious mind speaking. The unconscious part, however, struggles terribly with the loss of power and a sense of importance, however illusionary it was. There are a lot of perks that come with the CEO or President title, and many of the perks are all of a sudden out of financial range once we are no longer among the powerfully privileged. Worse, no one even notices the former CEO anymore, it's almost as though she or he has become invisible.

We all play various roles in our lives. For example, we may be a daughter and a sister. When we marry, we become a wife, a lover, and perhaps a mother. And so on. The hook is when we have identification that we perceive as being who we are. So the smiling baby becomes the nice little girl, having learned that "nice" makes Mommy and Daddy "happy." The growing daughter, perceiving her parents' expectations of her, learns how "smart" goes along with "nice," and she may become so identified with the persona of achieving that this becomes a permanent mask while she stifles what is really going on for herself.

It is when we are *attached to and involved with* the *identity* that it becomes pathological. For example, the yuppie woman becomes obsessed with her external appearance, which she identifies as being who she is. She's never seen in public without make-up on, hair looking good, skinny body poured into tight designer jeans or a dangerously short skirt, topped with blown-up breasts in an appropriate T-shirt or see-through shirt, Donald Duck lips, and lacquered extended fingernails that can click away on the table or extend the waving hand while making a point. Her obsession includes over-and-above workout schedules and daily weighing of herself upon waking lest there be a pound to spare.

Lordy-be if a tiny little roll emerges over those now one-size smaller jeans! Starvation is now required for at least two days! This perfect Barbie doll often is seen driving an expensive SUV and is wearing designer shades, of course. She has now become worthy of being seen as the perfect wife specimen to accompany her successful, good-looking husband.

This "successful" model certainly is not only for women. Plastic surgery among men has skyrocketed. Bicep implants, gluts maximized, six-pack abs implanted, hair coloring, and transplants to go along with the facelift to give a younger-than-I-am appearance. Men even accompany their wives for a discounted couples' Botox. Certainly, there is the belief that having a (by far!) younger woman on your arm shows just how virile and powerful you are–while the unconscious piece for most in this situation is the belief that the younger woman will keep them younger! The cosmic joke is that the desperate trying to keep up with the younger woman is actually aging!

Why do we think that our external appearance has anything to do with our authentic selves? What part of us wants to be identified with being younger than we are? Where has all this come from? Why such a need to *appear* powerful? In cases where these identifications have taken over, in the sense that the person actually believes they are their body, there is usually such a shut-down internally that any notion of looking at themselves in a more honest way is suppressed, submerged, and locked away in the depths of their interior. Yet there is truly more power in allowing the natural progression of the stages of life, and this includes aging and dying. This is an integral part of the human experience.

The woman leaves home as mother and puts on her mask as doctor when she walks into her office. There, she is not mother or wife. When she leaves, in a healthy shift out of the role, she hangs up her doctor mask; indeed she removes her white coat and picks up the next mask. Perhaps she's meeting her lawyer husband for dinner, so lover might be what's up next. The lawyer husband has hopefully hung up his mask at the office door, otherwise he's not likely to play much of a lover role over dinner.

What's the difference in these masks? Well, there are the practical masks of everyday life, based on the role for the moment, such as becoming a chatty girlfriend when meeting a girlfriend for coffee, or a heady linear guy at a corporate meeting, presenting statistics the team has compiled. The difference lies in the involvement in the role. Healthily, the roles shift from one to the next without any attachment to the previous one, whereas when the identification has become deeply embedded into the belief of "this is who I am," it becomes pathological. Generally speaking, pathologies such as these will ultimately manifest in some physical form, with ailments ranging from perhaps lower back pain or a kinked neck to something far more serious.

Probing our beliefs so that we can begin to see how we are programmed in certain ways, hence choosing to become more aware, often leads us into the deeper bigger picture question of "Who am I?" or better said, "Who am I not?"

Is this bundle of false concepts—this "Me" identification that is made up from all the ways you've been told you must behave and how you are to live your life—is this false "Me" really who you are? From experience I can tell you that who you really are has always been there, way before and unrelated to any belief or concept, and certainly unrelated to the way you present yourself to the world. Your true nature hasn't been learned—your true nature has no rules and it has never not been there. Your true nature is where the ease, the joy, the peace, the love, the *is-ness* lives.

Experiencing your own awakening into that which is already there—and has always been there—creates a huge paradigm shift in your life. After that, everything changes.

When we see in ourselves how our only—yes, I said ONLY—limitation in life is through our belief systems, the bigger picture begins to be revealed. And what an amazing picture it is! Truth is then seen as being our own truth and not a repeated parrot truth. The unfolding of our life, when we look back in review, can now be seen as absolutely magical, with each piece a perfect fit into the mosaic of your unique being-ness. As we look back and see the perfection, we are able to be with "what is" instead of resisting "what is" and wanting to make life different. When it becomes clear that no one is to blame for any piece of our life, this allows a shift. The reaction toward someone or something becomes the gift that it is. Intuition becomes heightened by our self-realization of the internal guidance that directs our every move, even though the mind still feels the need to take credit for it.

CHAPTER SEVEN:

Futile Resistance

Confess your hidden faults

Approach what you find repulsive

Help those you think you cannot help

Anything you are attached to, let it go

Go to the places that scare you.

Padampa Sangye's instructions to Machig Labdron

According to Pooh, today is the best day. Love this day as though it is your last day and one day it will be. That may seem obvious, yet many of us want to make yesterday or tomorrow more appealing than today. What is it that we don't like about today? Why is it not our best day? What keeps us from simply being in today as it is? How do we want to make it different? We have the illusion that if we were able to make today different from what it actually is, our lives would be perfect.

Expectation is the pattern of disappointment. The roots of our dissatisfaction lie in our expectations, which come from our beliefs of how our life *should* be and hence how it should be different from what it is. Why else would there be dissatisfaction in the first place? Could we have dissatisfaction if we didn't have a belief around what we want to be changed? The question then becomes, what is it that makes what is in front of me something I don't want?

Right here we can see a resistance to that which is, can't we? "I don't want this, I want that." So if we resist today, meaning *whatever* is in front of us, what other things do we resist in our lives? Many people resist, in its very basic form, life itself. Although dissatisfaction may not have come to the surface to be expressed—because who wants to sound so ungrateful—it is nevertheless common that underneath the dissatisfaction is the feeling that my life really isn't *the way it is supposed to be*. We have myriad unconscious beliefs that have built up our expectations of what we should have. Indeed, some even say: "I deserve to have…" as though entitlement is theirs alone, regardless.

We hear people repeating phrases about going with the flow, so much so that we have reduced its power through such glib misunderstanding. "Just go with the flow" has become a commonplace unthinking response. Yet being present with that simple phrase can still lead to profound exploration. Let's try that: go with the flow of your life, now. Imagine yourself as a leaf floating down the river, sometimes bumping into the shore, sometimes getting caught in twigs and leaves, often being rushed through rapid water then hurtled over falls, moving forward without any say in the matter. Going with the flow of the river. No resistance, no justification, no explanation, no trying to make it other than what it is. You will not encounter the rock you bumped into back there again. It's that simple. Life is not a dress rehearsal; there are no repeats in the script. It really is just this moment as you pass, noticing (or not) the rocks, the trees on the shore, the fish in the river.

When we can be with *what is*, life on Earth becomes the Heaven so many people seek. Conversely, some say that Hell is in living life from the place of wanting it to be different from what it is. As Brugh Joy would say, "All pain is resistance to where the soul wants to go." Unlike the leaf floating, simply allowing, the resistance is akin to trying to swim back up that river, back to that rock to see it all over again, back to enjoy the beams of sunlight that you remember shining on the silvery scales of the fish resting in that little quiet pool before the rapids. Feel the tension of the muscles as you try to swim against the current, struggling, straining, stressing to go upstream in the opposite direction to the natural flow of the river. Doesn't it feel exhausting just reading this? Yet this is what we are really doing when we resist life as it is, when we don't think our life is going the way it ought to and we are going to change it.

We are filled with resistances and these create our suffering. "Oh, Man, know Thyself and thou shalt know the Universe and the Gods." (The phrase inscribed in the ancient Temple of Delphi). Yet the source of much resistance is around knowing ourselves, and instead of being comfortable with all of who we are, we try to keep hidden all these secret pieces of ourselves, believing that if someone discovered just how awful we *really* are they would disown us. The cosmic joke (well, not *the* cosmic joke, because there are many) is that we all carry the same potential within ourselves. I am you and you are me. There is nothing to hide, nothing to disown. The gift comes from claiming all the pieces of potential that live within you. Once everything is okay—once the good, the bad, the right, the wrong, the beautiful, the ugly are all the same, so there is no charge to either pole—the freedom is yours. Peace, joy, ease with life just the way it is make for Heaven on Earth.

Instead, however, we have our beliefs, which give us our judgments around how our life is supposed to be. The "*supposed to be*" is uniquely ours. It is not our soul's desire, nor does it have anything whatsoever to do with anyone or anything else. It is simply made up of a bunch of idealistic beliefs that have come from others outside of ourselves outlining what life is supposed to be like. It's amusing to see how many people religiously say: "Thy will be done" when it would be more truthful for them to add, "As long as it is my way." It's a lie often spoken, because the reality is that the suffering comes from not understanding "Thy will be done."

When I think of the hook of how life is supposed to look, I recall a client who was considering a divorce. Of course, life put a perfect catalyst in front of her in the form of another man. The grass definitely did begin to look greener with the catalyst in the picture. He moved her from just talking and thinking about getting a divorce to actually starting the process. Then once the process was in motion, the catalyst took himself out of the picture. Don't you love it?

In a conversation before she started the divorce process, I was discussing and reviewing with her what a divorce would look like, having been there a couple of times myself. I asked, "And what if this means you will never again have a relationship?" She was furious with this question. Nevertheless, the point had been made, which is that projecting into the future according to our wants is not going to cut it with the forces of life.

Indeed, life has not gone as she had planned. As soon as the divorce was in motion and the good-package catalyst was gone, no one else showed up on the horizon. A facelift not for the faint of heart was the next attempt to force what this client wanted. That still didn't bring forth the "Knight in Shining Armor" to take care of her financially, nor did the Donald Duck lips nor the next face-lift. Friends who wanted to tell her: "Enough, enough, you're changing your natural beauty," said nothing because the defense wall was too big to allow any comment in. Nothing in her life changed, even though she felt she looked ter-rific. What did she have to do next to get a relationship?

Although we can say we know that life unfolds in spite of us, actually living with that as our truth is another story. In the case of wanting a relationship, it's as though we are saying, "Hey look, God, I know life is the way it needs to be, but I just want to point out to you that you've made a mistake. I'm *supposed to* have a relationship. I'm *not supposed to* be alone and I *deserve* to have someone take care of me."

Do we actually think "God" needs our help in designing our lives? Did Divine Source ask humankind what kind of planet they would like, and did we lowly beings participate in its creation? We see all sorts of very religious people praying to their personal "God" to make things different, because they don't want the discomfort of looking at what is in front of them. Although gratitude may receive mention from some people, more often the prayer becomes one of asking for change. "Please take away this, please give me that..."

As I see it, God really doesn't care whether or not you like what's in your hand dealt. On examination of my life, and others' lives, it appears we have a life-script that has been written without our assistance. Characters come and go in our movie, leading to the gift of our experiences, offering us the opportunity time and again for awareness.

Denial is common among those who want to "look better." I have another client who *really* doesn't want *anyone*—and the big piece is that this includes herself—to know she has done anything to her appearance, hence the need to lie even to herself. The lie is pervasive to the point that even her partner has been deceived into believing this is her "natural" look. Ask her directly if there has been any cosmetic assistance and you will receive an indignant: "Absolutely not."

We are living in an era of dissatisfaction. Surgically or cosmetically altering the way we look has become commonplace; I'm just using these stories as a good way to talk about this era. Marketing has been aimed at both women and men, all with the intent to create a feeling of inadequacy or wanting, a place of not being good enough. Instead of women's breasts being honored by women as a part of their nurturing femininity, they have bought into those marketing campaigns aimed at leaving young women feeling dissatisfied with their physical appearance. Their breasts are too big or too small or too saggy or too inverted. It seems their bodies have not been asked the question of how it feels to be so not good enough. Many men feel the same as these many women, believing that if they can alter their exterior and, as they see it, in this way become more appealing to others, they will also alter who they are inside. They ignore the old adage: "Beauty is only skin deep," and fall into the "Mirror, mirror on the wall," trap. The many arguments in favor of plastic surgery by those who have had it, or desire it, is that they are doing it for themselves. That's nothing more than their unclaimed defense accompanied by their self-seductive justification. Yes, true, they are doing it for themselves so that they will then see, in the mirror, someone who is more beautiful than the self-judgment of before and therefore more *acceptable* both to themselves and to others. Yet, it is what is underlying their need—the "why" it is so important—that begs to be asked and where the juicy answers lie.

Regardless, needing to willfully change our looks to look younger is a resistance to the way we are. I have that piece, too. I'm pleased I look younger than my age, and I might very well have a different perspective on this subject if I didn't or if I had what my mother used to call a "turkey neck." I have often looked at myself in the mirror, lifting here and there as if it were a facelift, noticing how much "better" I would look, yet immediately I get a huge "no" from my body just from thinking about it. So I notice my resistance to growing older and then thank my body for being healthy and alive. Trying to deny aging becomes the resistance to *looking* older, as if this illusion will actually alter aging itself.

A few people do go through their own process before having cosmetic surgery or injections, by honestly facing aging, and sitting with both their fears of it and their resistance to it. I've known only two people who were willing to drop into the place of honestly claiming their reason for altering their looks, which is quite small relative to the number of people I know who have had cosmetic surgery. Both of these individuals had successful and natural looking results along with fast healing.

As an aside to this conversation about cosmetic surgery, in working in energy medicine, scars and adhesions often come up. We have twelve major (and many more minor) meridians running through our body, ten of which have organs associated with them. Although the existence of these energy lines has been known for hundreds of years, they have only recently been acknowledged within conventional medical circles in the West. A well-healed scar is a thin white line; if the scar is red or has an adhesion, a thickness, this is an indication of a blockage of the energy flow across a particular meridian. I have had many fascinating experiences in working with scars. One thing I began to notice is that the attitude or, better said, the reason behind the surgery of the person appears to play a role in recovery. A friend who had a breast reduction because she didn't like her large breasts, finding them unfeminine and in the way, had many post-operative complications and very slow healing. Women who have breast implants because of feeling inadequate or not beautiful enough owing to their small breasts, will also often experience slow healing, which may be accompanied by breasts that remain forever tender and untouchable.

Regardless of how we want to look at this, the question remains: who are you in your attitude toward aging? Where is your resistance to aging? What are you afraid of about aging? What is it in our society that has made aging undesirable and to be avoided? What has happened that aging is not viewed with a sense of worth and a respect for the wisdom of having lived life? Why is it that so many women and men feel driven to have plastic surgery so that they can appear younger, believing it will have an impact on their lives?

We see both men and women being rejected in their work because of their age. We see men seeking younger women rather than looking more closely at their own age group. We see ad after ad showing a slim athletic body. What is it that drives a woman to starve and berate herself for having gained a few pounds just because her partner no longer finds her attractive *even though* she remains very slim—just not slim enough for him?

There is a wonderful singer I know who had breast implants and then developed breast cancer. She defended her decision to have implants by saying, "But I can't possibly be a singer without having some breasts to look sexy." Really? When did this pathological external reference start? I used to think of my mother and her friends as "Betty Crocker women," who strove to look perfect to the outside world. The internal process appears to have been lost along the centuries as the religious screws for controlling women tightened and women lost their sense of self. The masculine was calling the shots on who women were to be, as it had been for centuries. And I felt this as a child, being raised by a woman whose values, I feel sad in saying, tended to be outside herself.

Things have shifted in that women (and men who are in touch with their feminine side) are standing up now, in their feminine power. Around the world, women are saying "No!" No to the linear, analytical, external masculine; no to the masculine that wants to keep women controlled; no to the masculine that creates the wars and conflicts, killing sons of women; no to the masculine that mutilates and rapes women for their satisfaction; no to the masculine that kills animals in an attempt to get an erection; no to the masculine that allows the inequality on the planet; no to the masculine that deems the external material world as being of most value; and no to the masculine that is destroying our precious planet Earth.

The bottom line is that we seem to be in resistance to the natural process of life. Aging doesn't mean you become old and sedentary just because you are a certain age; that's a useless belief. On the contrary, someone who is content with life as it is generally has a vitality and longevity that others do not. I am thinking of several woman who are in their eighties as I write this and who are more active in creating change than they've ever been. In keeping with that, it also seems we are seeing more honoring of the wisdom of people in their later years. I've noticed that many younger adults are showing a reverence that earlier generations did not, seeking advice and guidance from elders who can share their earned life wisdom. The beauty of those who are joyful with simply being in life shines through from the inside out. Regardless of elders' external appearance, their beauty cannot be bought or created. "Please don't retouch my wrinkles; it took me so long to earn them," said Italian actress Anna Magnani.

It is said that when everything is stripped away, existential fear remains and is the last piece to be let go of. Existential fear is that which relates to the "Me" actually being a "Me." "What will happen to me when I die?" However, the "Me" has nothing to do with the true nature of who each person is. The "Me" is the illusion formed from all of our beliefs. Through an awakening-process exercise, we can experience being fully in that which has always been, that which never dies, the spaciousness where "Me" does not exist. When we cease to resist, we liberate that pattern within the context of spaciousness. Although this may be a fleeting experience, we now have a term of reference from having experienced Presence.

We resist feeling into the death of our small self. This is often a buried sub-conscious piece that keeps self-exploration at bay, because when we do choose to delve deeply into our internal caves, there is constant dying to these false pieces of "Me." We begin dying to ourselves, to pieces of ourselves, to the illusion that our personality—our masks—has anything to do with our higher Self. In its own odd way, hanging on to these beliefs feels comfortable whereas examining them and shifting our perspective on them can feel threatening.

Many years ago, I decided to do an exercise with myself in which I imagined myself dying. I immersed myself in dying. I felt myself dying. I imagined my family and friends saying goodbye to me, wondering what they would say about me. I stayed in this process, fully feeling my dying as much as I could, for three days. It was of interest to me that on the second night I absolutely could not sleep. Not at all. If I went to sleep, I could die, my mind said. Hearing how elderly people often don't sleep long or deeply made sense to me then: unconsciously there is a knowing that they may not wake up.

There are probably as many theories as there are people as to what happens when our physical body quits functioning. Some theories feel more plausible, perhaps, yet we need to consider that the reason they do may be because they fit more closely with our beliefs about the after-life. In being absolutely truthful, however, we have to be willing to acknowledge that whatever ideas or theories we have about the after-life are only that and built on the beliefs of others. We ourselves have not had the experience of physically dying, and therefore we do not know what—if anything—occurs after life. Near-death experiences (NDEs) are *near* death, not death of the physical body. All I know is that I do not know.

I remember when an aunt of mine died, though. The nurse called to say the time was near, but by the time I got to the hospital she had already passed on a few minutes prior. As I held her hand and silently finished my goodbye, there was an audible "swoosh" sound. For me, it was the essence of this soul leaving the temple of the body. While the physical body deteriorates into dust, to be blown away by any wind, the essence, consciousness itself, appears to continue. In having had my own experiences, as opposed to a religious belief around death, my perspective suggests a continuation of our essence. I know of a few doctors who have had similar experiences and conclusions, and there are many references to this continuation in various ancient texts, described in both auditory and sensory terms.

Yet while there is still identification with the body—in other words, of actually believing that the body, how it looks, how it functions, actually has anything to do with who you truly are—there is the fear of what happens to the false "Me" when I die.

There is no light without shadow and no psychic wholeness without imperfection. To round itself out, life calls not for perfection but for completeness; and for this the 'thorn in the flesh' is needed, the suffering of defects without which there is no progress and no ascent.

C. G. Jung, Complete Works, Vol. 12, 208

Carl Jung, the famous Swiss psychiatrist, said that whatever you deny about yourself, the resistance, like a dragon, will sneak up and hit you from behind. Succinctly said: that which you resist persists. What Jung meant by the dragon is that all internal pieces desire to be expressed or acknowledged, as in bringing them into conscious awareness. When denied or unconscious, they *will* find a sideways form of expression. I don't know if you remember the incident in Colombia when a slew of American secret service agents were caught soliciting prostitutes, doing drugs, and checking out porn? When we are in resistance, it means we want to see only one pole while the other pole is stuffed down into the unconscious, closely guarded so that no one finds out they have these "awful" pieces in them.

For these guys, their job demanded a certain decorum along with strict requirements. They were expected to be hyper-alert at all times, observant of everyone and everything around them, while being held accountable for high-level security. That's one pole. The other pole was where they were attracted to people who would be high-security risks, while not giving a crap about anyone or anything. The imbalance crunch came when they identified with their roles as security agents, one of the poles, to such a degree that they were security themselves. This was their total identification. In keeping with that, they denied their attraction to the opposite pole, to the illegal and dangerous, to the very security risks they were trained to stop—the abuses of porn, prostitutes, drugs, alcohol, or whatever fed the denied pieces they refused to acknowledge. Again, what we resist persists. In this way, the dragon slapped them from behind when they were unconsciously unaware of the dark-side demons that were demanding acknowledgment. It's all quite beautiful how life set up their role identifications so perfectly. Having this be one group we would absolutely not expect to go against the law, and in doing that risking the security of the President of the United States, is quite delicious.

Jung was the one who coined the phrase "The Shadow," which also often gets referred to as "the dark side." "The Shadow" is elusive–we can't catch our shadow. In consciousness terms, it consists of the dark, unsavory, unwanted pieces that we unconsciously want to keep hidden because we don't want anyone to know they are a part of us. It appears, however, that wholeness can come only from our claiming all that is. What exists in you exists in me. What existed in Hitler, Saddam Hussein, or any other "bad" guy exists in me and in you. This doesn't mean this is who I am, nor does it mean that I act on these pieces. It does mean I need to claim the pieces as part of who I am. So, for example, I am not a murderer by nature. It would be a lie, however, if I were to deny I could ever be a murderer, because I can imagine several scenarios in which I could actually kill someone. I wouldn't turn against my neighbor to save my own skin, yet I can imagine the possibility.

We want to be seen in the way we consider favorable, and we want our unsavory pieces to stay hidden. In the life scheme, however, hiding produces the opposite because it is in the denial, in the resistance, that the suffering exists. I remember years ago being in a circle with a couple. Included in his bucket pulled from the sea of consciousness was "The Pedophile." To satisfy this driving desire, he was a Cubs or Scouts leader so he could be around little boys. At the time of working in the circle, he said he had not yet acted on this but described what a powerful force it was for him. And he was understandably afraid of the power.

As the group worked with this force, his wife came to understand the dynamics of it and agreed to help him through role-playing. When "The Pedophile" would come forward, when it would take him over, his wife gave him permission to act it out with her while she played the role of a young boy. How are you in reading about this? Are you able to do so from a spiritually mature perspective or is there a reaction in you?

Let's take a look at how we resist ourselves. In honest self-examination, what don't you like about yourself? What are your secrets? What do you want to be different in you or your life? How many times do you drop into the place of feeling not good enough and wanting to be someone other than who you are? I'm talking about even seemingly small insignificant things. For example, I used to feel envy, true envy, for people with a huge head of thick wavy hair, along with a serious wish for it. "Hair?" you say, "what's the big deal about thick, luscious hair?" Believe me, only someone with that kind of hair would ask such a dumb question. Big hair makes anyone look positively gorgeous every morning with no need for an immediate shower, shampoo, and blow dry. Instead, I have my fine hair, which leaves me looking less than stunning some mornings, and requires attention every morning. Throw in the Slavic hips instead of the slender French ones that I really want, and I'm on the way to dissatisfaction and resistance to the way I look. Anyone out there who can identify with what I've just said?

Okay, so I'm making light of a piece I don't like about myself, and my truth is that there were a number of things I would have liked to change about my body. Now I thank my wonderful body that serves me so well and just acknowledge when I judge parts of it. My bitch became my friend years ago. I am often jealous of certain friends and look at my possessiveness piece in the eye. My Princess, bless her, no longer rules my actions now that she's been given her space.

So we set ourselves up in this way, with our beliefs piled high, as to who we are supposed to be and, more specifically, how our life is supposed to be. And believe me, this can make people very ill. Here's a poignant example from another client. If you were looking from the outside, you would say she belonged to the ideal family. First, her parents had two children—her brother, who was born first, and then her, which everyone knows is the perfect order. The parents have a solid marriage. They have enviable financial stability. Both the kids were good students and therefore went to the very best of private schools, continuing on to the very best universities.

This young woman, of course, met the ideal man. He came dressed as a successful professional. His family was particularly well connected socially, which added a new and perfect ingredient to the ideal mix. This ideal woman married this ideal man and they had the most exquisite, perfect wedding. Before too long, their first child was born and it was … a boy, of course. Two years later, in perfect timing, their daughter was born.

This woman, so unconsciously steeped in the beliefs of the ideal family, created her own ideal family, just like the one she had been raised in. Then one day, while her daughter was still a baby, the now even more successful husband came home with divorce papers. Although this would be devastating for anyone, for this woman it translated out to a serious health threat within a couple of months. The lungs energetically hold on to grief and are also related to our letting go versus wanting to hang on to the trappings of the story. In this woman's case, one lung collapsed, her other lung was functionally below optimal, and her hemoglobin level plummeted. In other words, she was in big trouble. As it happened, I was going to be in the city where she lived, the day after I found out about this. I offered and did two energy-medicine (BodyTalk) sessions on this woman over two days. As you can probably guess, much of what came up in the sessions was around beliefs, grief, and the collapse of her ideal life. The pathology of the beliefs specifically relating to her failure to meet her ideal family expectations, resulting in this current physical manifestation, appeared to have been released. Within a couple of days, both her lungs were functioning beautifully and her hemoglobin was at the highest level she had ever had.

So when I say that beliefs and our health cannot be separated, this case and others like it are what have been my experience.

Bigger than our addiction to plastic surgery from resistance to aging, we are a nation of anti-depressant users. Women are larger users than men, although the use among men appears to be rising. The overall use of anti-depressants in the Western world has skyrocketed since the late 1990s, with a dramatic increase in the early part of this century. The nature of anti-depressants is to flatten out the natural undulations of our emotions so that we lose the highs and lows, but then everything feels more or less the same.

If people are less than happy, they have been made to believe that something is wrong with them for feeling the way they are feeling. It's the "Be Happy" craze, as if a successful life is about being happy. And the craziness of buying into this belief isn't even noticed by most people. The resistance to allowing whatever we are feeling by simply feeling may be viewed by some as "being too emotional" or "self-indulgent" or "weak." In teaching energy medicine, I remind participants that we need to look at *dis-ease* (be it physical, mental, or spiritual) from both the physical and energetic viewpoints. So, for example, in the situation with the woman whose lung collapsed when faced with divorce, the physical was the collapse of her lung while the energetic was partly the holding on to her grief and pain from loss.

Chemical imbalances can result in depression and related symptoms. Energetically, when chemical imbalance is not the issue, I see depression as a suppression, a depressing of what is wanting to be acknowledged or expressed. Emotions are a natural part of being human, and we are constantly feeling as we go through our experiences. We move from one emotion to the next without any conscious awareness of them until there is something that grabs our attention. Then we either acknowledge what we are feeling, whether it is spontaneously arising or from an event, or we try to suppress it, to ignore it so that we do not have to deal with it.

One of the stumbling blocks for many people is emotions themselves. We judge them and determine that some are "good," such as feeling happy or carefree, while others—particularly anger—are "bad" and not to be expressed. Just what exactly makes one emotion "good" while another emotion is "bad"? An emotion is simply a movement of energy—it rises and it falls. Projected anger, which means pointing a blaming finger at someone else, is different from feeling angry. Feeling anger as an experience can be a great motivator, a mover and a shaker. Physically, this can translate to unblocking an artery or releasing a bowel. Energetically, it can get the internal creative fire burning. So why do we make anger "wrong"? If you do some honest self-exploration, are you able to see that you might hold some fear around your own anger? Do you feel afraid that if you actually expressed your anger you could harm someone? Going back to Jung, it is exactly the suppressed and repressed emotion that allows the "dragon" to hit you with it when least expected. Healthy expression of anger is not projected out on anyone, nor does it need to be about something or someone. Anger, just like any other emotion, does not have to have a reason; it just rises. "I feel angry!" is simply awareness of an emotion with the frequency of anger. "I'm so mad at you!" is projection out on the other person, blaming them for "making" you angry. Just owning your own anger, expressing it from what you are feeling, can be very juicy and very sexy. Projected anger, on the other hand, will feel threatening.

Let's say I am in a relationship and I ask my partner what's bothering him. My partner refuses to engage me, to give me anything of himself, and instead withholds expression of what he is feeling. He then is energetically saying, "I will not give you what you want from me." That will most likely stir anger in me, whether I identify it within myself at the time or not. On the other hand, if he expresses his anger, staying in his body with it and certainly without any projection or physical attack of any sort, I will feel excited because of his honest communication and also from the big energy of anger being expressed. Unfortunately, we have become accustomed to suppressing our emotions, so that when we explode, like the cap off the toothpaste, it is really about held-onto resentments that haven't yet been expressed.

Another of the stumbling blocks in looking at emotions, is that we assume there needs to be a reason behind the emotion. Yet the emotion is simply arising. When I was a child, my mother would often be distressed and concerned because she would perceive me as being sad and therefore thought something was wrong. I can remember, however, that it had nothing to do with anything in particular being wrong; it was just the way I felt at the time. Although I did not have the words to describe what I was feeling at this stage of my life, I can relate to this now as sadness and at times overwhelming grief. I remember how they would just overtake me. There was no reason for my sadness or grief. I did not have an abusive or deprived childhood. I was just feeling sad. Yet, in our society, we don't want to see that. We judge sadness as indicating that something is "wrong" and therefore needs to be fixed. When we see someone crying, we unconsciously, or perhaps at times knowingly, want to break the energy, so we give them a hug or pat them on the back while telling them that it's okay to cry. We think we are being compassionate, yet underlying our action is an attempt to prevent our own discomfort. The hug or pat on the back cuts into the person's energy field and immediately stops their process, while telling them it's all okay is a judgment. Now the interesting part of that is the question behind why we want to stop them from crying. What is wrong with feeling sad and crying? What is it that is being stirred in us when we see someone cry? We don't want to feel our own sadness in this case, or perhaps we don't want to give in to our own desire to sit and cry because we perceive that as being weak. How is it that crying or feeling sad or being depressed are viewed as something to be judged or turned into a big deal?

If I say to a friend, "I'm feeling so lonely today and I can't stop crying," I am simply asking to be seen and heard. I don't want you to try and take away my sadness or make everything okay. I'm just sad. Or it may be "I'm afraid to be alone," and when I can allow myself to feel that fear, this piece of my humanness, the power of trying to keep it hidden melts away. I mentioned earlier that when we fully feel what we are feeling, when we sit in this space regardless of the discomfort, the feeling will morph into a place of calmness or even joy. In contrast, denying what is there simply stores it energetically in the body. Once a lot of unaddressed energy has been stored, it will then manifest in some external form.

I find it of great interest that the Mormon state of Utah has the highest rate of anti-depressant use in the United States, because I see the Mormon women as being suppressed by the men of their church. This may not be true for all Mormon women, and I also realize that Mormon women do not share my point of view and I appreciate their perspective. Yet, from what I have experienced, their husbands appear to have great freedom to do and be as they like, whereas the women are expected to be obedient, well behaved, moral, and hard-working, and to be happy because they are obeying. There are such strong beliefs within this religion, as in most religions, that to challenge them wouldn't happen for anyone who adheres to the teachings. So although I know some absolutely wonderful Mormon women, women I love as friends and who are open to self-exploration in general, nevertheless, I see these beliefs as a major block. From my perspective, given that Utah is a Mormon state and given that the use of anti-depressants is what it is there, I imagine there is a direct correlation between the tightly held-on-to beliefs and mental health issues. *Whatever beliefs we hold onto as being true are our blinders.*

I do realize this is a delicate subject, yet given that I have made the above comments, I am going to include here an actual case to support, in part, what I have just said. How typical this is I can't say, except that this is not the first I have heard of women being banned by the Mormon church for their behavior. In contrast, I have not heard of a similar occurrence for a man, even though I do know of various situations similar to the one presented here. As with anything, in this book or elsewhere, if you are triggered you might consider it an opportunity to explore what's under your trigger.

This man held a prestigious position in law and was an elder of the Mormon Church. His wife also had a career. The couple had eight children, and she served a minimum of fourteen people for dinner every night. Although Mormon women do seem to take it in stride, I personally find that a staggering thought. My point in mentioning this, however, is that the woman also held a job outside the home in addition to one heck of a big job at home.

This elder of the Church had, shall we say, a taste for sex and expressed it through constant affairs. The woman had been considering leaving the marriage because of these affairs and, in the process she had a very short fling with some guy. During an argument with her husband, she threw this at him. You guessed it, the husband was furious. How dare she! Now remember, he had had multiple affairs throughout his marriage to this woman. He was an elder in the church, while she had also been deemed good enough to attend the same level of church services as his honorable self. In retaliation for her confession of having had a fling, he exposed her to the church members by standing up and telling the entire congregation. She was declared a sinner and banned from the church. One of her sons was about to get married in that same church in a couple of weeks and now she would be unable to attend. The question I am raising here is that when we have suppressive rules that demand we behave in a certain way, what happens to that which is not allowed to be expressed?

Interestingly, the website fairmormon.org, in addressing the issue of depression, states: "While Utah does have the highest rate of anti-depressant use in the United States, there is no evidence that this is because of stress from the LDS lifestyle and culture. Credible research has shown that LDS women are actually more likely to identify themselves as 'happy' than non-Mormon women. Religion generally (and the LDS religion specifically) has been repeatedly shown to be either beneficial or neutral for mental health and well-being." Well, that statement makes me feel depressed.

There is enormous freedom in being okay with who you are. Feelings (a bodily sensation—"I feel heavy in my heart") and emotions that accompany them (a frequency that we give a name to—"I feel sad") will not kill you, but suppression of them just might. What we are feeling is *our* feeling, no one else's. No one caused it and no one else is responsible for your feeling. It is yours to claim, or not. Hopefully, by the end of this book, you will be okay with what is, without the need to change what is in front of you, and be able to enjoy the peace and ease that comes from it.

I will share with you a couple of pieces of myself that, to be honest, I'd really rather not. However, I did make a commitment to myself and I will honor my truth-telling. And, as Hamlet expressed, "There is nothing either good or bad, but thinking that makes it so."

My mother, as you've already read, desperately wanted me to be the nice, well-behaved little girl. My brother was nine years older and the love of my mother, while I was the apple of my father's eye. Our parents had some friends over and I imagine I was feeling as though I wasn't getting the attention I wanted. I was only five at the time, and although I have suppressed the immediate "why" behind my action, I have no doubt it is what drove that action. I pushed my brother down the basement stairs and watched him tumble down. My mother, of course, screamed, and everyone was concerned. Once it was determined that my brother was not seriously hurt, the attention turned to me. "Oh, she's only a child!" "She didn't mean to do it." "It was an accident." What I do recall is that I was saying to myself, "Oh yes, I did mean to push him." I wanted him out of the way, and I felt bad and evil for my desires. Nowadays I can have compassion for this little girl and how she made herself feel for doing such a terrible thing. I can have compassion for my brother, as I imagine that he felt hurt by my action while probably suppressing even the idea that I had purposely pushed him. My brother's gone now, and I never did say I was sorry to him. Besides, that would have been a lie because it was intentional. I would, however, have liked to have acknowledged it by talking about it.

Have you ever had a thought you weren't proud of? One where you wanted to deny that it had even been in your mind? Have you ever watched yourself do something that another part of "you" didn't want to do? What does the saying "I am of two minds" mean? Where do your thoughts come from? No one knows the answer to that other than *thoughts happen*. We even say: "something popped into my mind just now." So the thought happens *and then* thinking occurs, based on our filters. We will either become involved with our thinking or not.

I was in South Africa, working with a group around beliefs. As I was talking about secrets and the things we don't want people to know about ourselves, I acknowledged something I had never admitted to anyone. It was difficult to remember this and more so to own it publicly. When I was in my last marriage—terrified at the very thought of being on my own, wondering how I would survive financially—I would often wake in the morning hoping my husband had died. This would solve everything! I would have financial freedom and I would be rid of him. I can even remember a couple of moments in which I considered what I might be able to do to hasten that possibility. Thanks be, this was not in my script or, perhaps more accurately said, it was a detour I had enough awareness to avoid.

We fear these pieces of ourselves. We can feel the power as we resist them. The irony is that when we claim our dark, smelly, repulsive parts, their power is completely taken away. The dragon no longer can come and smack us from behind. There is no power once the judgment is gone. And even though we think that acknowledging these unkind, unwanted, unsavory parts could kill us, the contrary is what happens, and life begins to flower in an unexpected way.

Resistance tires us and bogs us down. Resistance is more than futile, it is destructive. We can be so terribly unkind to ourselves—cruel, really—through our self-judgment. The only reason we judge others is because of this self-judgment; others are simply a mirror for us to see ourselves in. So be kind to yourself and know that there is nothing in you—no thought, no matter how evil you may think it to be—that others do not have also.

Divine speaks

in many ways,

Reminding

There is only now.

The earth shakes

I feel the panic, pain

My heart breaks

My tears of no help.

No plan holds

As the illusion crumbles

Reminding, reminding

There is only now.

Drop to silence

Sending love and blessings.

Beverly Lutz

CHAPTER EIGHT:

In the Beginning was the Story

May you awaken to the mystery of being here and enter the quiet immensity of your own presence.

John O'Donohue

In the beginning was the story. It's as simple as that. We continually create stories that make us feel alive and involved, then we use them as a means of seeing our own life and life in general. They are our own little created drama, a part of our life-movie. And by golly do we ever like them! Without them, life would seem boring for those still caught in them. Without the story there is no history, there is no chewing on and repeating events over and over, trying to make sense of them, and there is no hanging on to the blame of how, who or what harmed us or ruined our lives.

We are the writers of the story, and what we write is based, like everything else, on our filters, which give us our unique perceptions. Using a simple true example, let's look at two people who go out on their first date. They had met online, had done a couple of visual calls on the computer, and now this was their first physical meeting. Each is feeling slightly nervous, then both are quickly and pleasantly surprised as they relax into a wonderful evening. When they part, the man says he will call the woman the next day so they can make plans for another date.

Tomorrow comes and there is no call. The woman now starts to go into her self-doubt questions around men who can't be trusted—men who never do as they say—and then finally into the place of wondering what she has done wrong. By the end of day two she has gone over in her head every single thing she said that evening, including what she ordered for dinner (was it too expensive? was it the second glass of wine she had?), and then questioning and chastising herself. "Oh, I shouldn't have said that." "I knew I shouldn't have been so open on our first date, and now he's not interested." Despair is the name of the game by the end of day three, and she is now convinced that this was all her fault because she hadn't behaved "properly," including her now-list of shouldn't-haves.

Ten days have gone by when she receives a phone call from this man. "Please don't hang up," he implores, after hearing her terse "yes" in reply to his warm hello. He goes on to tell her what happened in his life when he got home from their date. He had a message from his desperate mother telling him that his dad had just had a heart attack and could he please come home. Checking flights he found there was a red-eye that he could just make if he left his home immediately, and this flight would put him in his parents' city by early morning. He quickly grabbed a couple of things and was out the door, driving himself as fast as he could to the airport to ensure he didn't miss this flight. It was only once he had settled himself into his seat on the plane, relaxing a bit knowing that he was at least on his way to his dad, that he realized he did not have this woman's telephone number with him. He hadn't brought his computer, where her number was in an email message, leaving him with no way to reach her because her phone number was un-listed.

So now we have the real story of why he hadn't called. The one of interest here, however, is the story she created, all of which was done from her place of beliefs about men, her own sense of unworthiness, and the nobody-loves-me kind of place.

I've done the same thing myself, more times than I care to remember—little stories about why someone didn't invite me somewhere when they were inviting mutual friends; nobody loves me; why I haven't received a reply to my email or why hasn't someone returned my call? A part of my mosaic includes a piece of fear of being left out, or of being left behind, and I used to have dreams about both of them.

Another client's mosaic included major issues of father abandonment and idealism around being financially rescued so that her life could be more secure, interesting, and glamorous than it was. Although she had become aware of these dynamics to a degree, there was nevertheless a strong resistance to owning them. Her defense was strong. How this translated out in her life was that she would seek people with money and create friendships with them by being a syrupy, nice, "loving" person. Her illusion was that these well-connected friends would introduce her to their friends and in this way she would find her rescuer. In the process, her internal prostitute, albeit unconscious to her, was vigilant and active, because she was not able to be herself with these people and she was selling a piece of herself by not being in her truth. She remained on guard, protecting the image, the identification, she created. The whole thing still back-fires on her every time she has a date because of her own unclaimed dynamics. She creates unbelievable stories around the event and in desperation to be rescued turns the evening into "dating" when it's no such thing. Having a one-night stand does not create a relationship, yet she doesn't see it that way.

To repeat, the story is just a story. The past is just a story. Once you know that, the power is gone and there is no need to repeat the story. My story is mine, seen through my eyes, through my filters of beliefs, through my unique colored glasses. What triggers me about a story is most likely to be different from what triggers you in the same story. In fact, looking at an event, it's likely there will be no trigger for anyone but me or, in your case, for anyone but you. Remember that the trigger, the button pusher, the external person or event, is there for you as an invitation to explore your inner chambers. Then it's what we do with the story, how we hang on to the story, how we are involved with the story. My brother was a great one for holding on, no matter how old the story, he could be like the puppy who will not let go of the sock. And I need to remind myself as I remember him, *just like me.*

"I will not forgive you, no matter what. I will take this to my grave." And so people do die with the energetic heaviness in their heart that comes from refusing to forgive the story. Indeed, the holding on to resentments, the heaviness in the heart, the closed heart can be a fuse for a major heart attack.

I was in Egypt a long time ago and bought, as many tourists do, several papyrus drawings, including a large one of the after-life. In ancient Egypt, it was a common painting in tombs and is called "The Weighing of the Heart." Paintings and their accompanying hieroglyphics told the stories of the mythology and lifestyle of those times. In this particular painting of the after-life, we can see that the heart is being weighed on one side of the scale against a feather on the other side of the scale. Anubis, protector of the deceased, is in charge of the scale and the weights, while Ibis the Scribe is noting the findings. Sobek, the crocodile god, is waiting to see if he will be devouring the heart. Osiris, masculine god of the underworld, is seated on his throne waiting for the results, while Hathor, the feminine, sits beside him. In this mythology, when the heart weighs lighter than the feather, the soul was said to be off the wheel of karma. In other words, the soul will have evolved back into pure consciousness once the veils of beliefs have been lifted and the realization has been reached that separation is only an illusion and there is nothing that we think of us as "Me."

When we hold on to resentments and old used-up tapes, they are energetically like heavy chains around our heart, as is our resistance to letting them go. As we become aware of and release some of these stories that no longer serve us, along with the resistance to do so, we find ourselves feeling lighter and freer as the weight is lifted. The heart feels lighter.

Innate Harmony, the peace beyond all understanding, is one of the attributes of the heart. It is the calm in the midst of chaos, the center of the spinning wheel, and that which makes the heart lighter than a feather. It is the still deep pool; it is the dharmakaya which constitutes the unmanifested, 'inconceivable' aspect of a Buddha, out of which Buddhas arise and to which they return after their dissolution, dissolved into the pool.

Brugh Joy, MD

The following is a poignant example of what it means when the heart lightens from the release of burdens, and also illustrating the magic of how life presents us with our next step. I had a client, who I will call Henry, who had cancer of the tongue. Although no illness is desirable, this one is really not pretty. The time I first saw him, I had a practice with a waiting list of many weeks. It was a Sunday evening when a client called, apologizing while explaining that she had just found out she couldn't make her appointment first thing the next morning. I rebooked her and then wondered who would show up in her place. Shortly after, the phone rang again with a man on the other end. He explained how he had received my name and that he was desperately calling on behalf of a friend. Was there any way I could see his friend immediately? It was urgent. I was able to tell him that *it just so happened* the first appointment of the day was now available. "My friend will take it!"

I opened the door to see a man whose energy indicated to me that he was very ill. Prior to my treatment, he explained about his cancer. I also learned that he was a strict born-again Christian. I mention that because, in any other circumstance, I imagine I would have been considered "evil" or a "witch" or, at the very least, not someone such a Christian would go to see. However, as he was clearly terrified of dying, he was willing to try anything and everyone. In our conversation, which included my questions about his life, he told me of his domineering wife. I'm sure you know the kind—the partner who interrupts all the time and finishes your sentence. I asked him then if he felt he had lost his voice. It was striking to me that here was a man who clearly had no interest in knowing anything about himself through any form of self-examination and who was willing to be told what to do by his wife, yet, upon hearing my question, without missing a beat, said, "Oh, yes, yes, that's true. I don't have a voice with my wife or with my colleagues. I don't even have a voice with my kids, and I didn't have a voice when I was a kid either."

During this first session, as we were about to start, his cell phone rang. Nervously grabbing it while telling me quickly that he simply had to answer it, he said hello. I could overhear the conversation.

"Henry," says this sharp, abrupt man, "where are you? You are supposed to be here."

"I'll be there shortly."

"Look," Mr. Abrupt says, "I need you to sign these papers now. I'm going out of town and I won't be back until Thursday."

"I'll be there shortly," my client says again. "I'll sign them then."

The conversation over, Henry now had a sickly color. "That was my surgeon. He wants to cut out my tongue on Friday. What should I do?" he asked. While I was raging internally over what was, for me, a grossly unethical proposal of mutilating surgery that would not save this man's life, I could say nothing. Instead I answered, "I can't tell you what to do, Henry. I can suggest you have some quiet time and listen to your internal guide for your answer." Then I started the session. When we finished, Henry sat straight up and in a firm strong voice said, "I am not going to have that surgery!" No sooner was that out of his mouth than he nervously added, "But what will my wife say?" My reply was, "This is your body, Henry. Just say you have decided against the surgery."

On the third visit, based on information that had come through in the BodyTalk session, I told him the following. "You were four years of age. Your mother punished you and your father never knew about it." What I didn't add is that this was related to his cancer, like a seed planted that grew from there. Lying on the table, with deer-in-the-headlight eyes looking at me, Henry said, "That is just the way it was, but I have never ever told anyone about it, not even my wife. My mother punished me and threw me into the cellar (one of the old-style cold dirt cellars). She turned off the light, locked the door, and I was terrified."

So now we have a scene of a four-year old boy, terrified both of the dark and of what might live in the cellar. The mother was furious with him and this time she was going to make him obey. Washing his mouth out with soap and spankings hadn't worked, but the cellar was going to do the trick. And what do you suppose had been the cause for Henry being punished this way? Have you guessed it? He had been a strong-willed child who, in the mother's paradigm, "talked back" to her, whereas in the child's paradigm he was just expressing and finding himself.

The next session was the last I saw of Henry before he died. When I opened the door to him that day I was taken aback by how well he looked. "Wow, Henry," I said, "I don't know what it is you are doing, but you look terrific!" His reply touched me deeply. "I know I am dying and I have never felt better in my life."

This is what it looks like when the heart is released from burdens that it has held on to. This is what happens as the chains are released. This is how it feels when the heart weighs less from the letting go of old stories, old tapes, long-held-onto resentments, and regrets.

My teacher Brugh Joy would always say, "Remember that healing does not equal a cure." This has proved to be one of the most invaluable pieces for me with my work in energy medicine. Healing is about the weighing of the heart. The chains of our beliefs weigh heavy, so when these held-on-to energies are released, there is a lightening. It is akin to a weight being lifted, and the person feels "better," less burdened, lighter. But we have our stories around curing, don't we? We think that if the disease hasn't been killed off, then nothing has happened. We have bought into the stories around health just as we have with other stories. I certainly took heed of one of my more profound experiences that I had from working at Hospice, with dying people and, in this case, with a specific woman. I was a licensed massage therapist at the time. In North America, it used to be that massage therapists were not allowed to give massages to people with cancer, because it was felt this would assist in spreading of the cancer cells, whereas in Europe massage and lymphatic drainage are some of the first recommended approaches to illness. This woman was in the final stages of lung cancer and, given her condition, her bed had to remain at a near-seated angle to assist with the fluid in her lungs. I was in her room, chatting with her this one day, and then asked if she would like a massage. As I was massaging her back, she began to cry, sobbing and sobbing as I worked on her. After she had released all that was coming up for her, she said, "I am so sad I had to get cancer in order to truly feel a human touch."

More often than not, the people I spoke with in Hospice expressed how cancer had been a gift—albeit an unsolicited one—in that it brought them into the place of cherishing life just as it is, without expectations or demands. There is a big story around cancer. The word alone brings up fear for most people, and out of this fear we buy into deadly treatments.

I had a client who used to love to have me talk about her in my classes. With her permission of course, I used her name and my students all knew her. They had become endeared to Agnes and her journey, so that every time I mentioned her name, sharing part of a session to use in teaching, I would see a room of smiles looking back at me. How Agnes showed up on my doorstep and became a character in my life-movie, and I in hers, is a magical story all on its own. What I want to mention here is related specifically to her cancer story. Agnes had primary breast cancer that had metastasized to her bones and liver, for which she had been treated with both chemotherapy and radiation. When I first saw her, she was in a great deal of pain and unable to sleep at night. Although she had been treated for a couple of years by a well-known cancer center, she had just been told, "We have done all we can for you. There is nothing more to be done. Go home, enjoy your family, and prepare for your death." They had given her a life guestimate of a few weeks. She was in her mid-50s. After our first BodyTalk session, Agnes was, in her words, "80 to 85% out of pain" and she slept through the night for the first time in many months. I continued seeing her regularly, during which time she refused all conventional cancer therapies. Given our healthcare system, however, she was required to go for regular check-ups to the cancer center. During these, the oncologists would chastise her for not continuing with treatment while, at the same time saying, "Look, whatever it is you're doing, just keep on doing it, because your cancer is not behaving the way *it is supposed to.*" Several sites on her spine were now gone, the liver appeared almost healthy, and there was no sign of further growth or metastasis.

Fast forward six and a half years—yes, years, not months. I was leaving that evening on a long trip. As is my habit, I still had many things to do. Yet a persistent voice inside me kept telling me to call Agnes. I hadn't seen her for a couple of months because of my traveling. She was delighted to chat, saying also she had been planning on calling me because she wasn't feeling well but thought I was traveling. One of the things she said that day was: "I want to thank you for all these six and a half years. I know you will say you didn't have anything to do with it, and I understand, but I still want to thank you for this time. When I first came to see you, I was so terrified at the thought of dying. Now, I want you to know, I am totally at peace, with no fear. These years have been the most significant of all my life." She talked further about how the many shifts she experienced within had translated to shifts with all her relationships, especially those with family members. Agnes had experienced a healing and it had nothing to do with a cure. Her heart was lighter and she was now OK with dying, if that was in the hand dealt to her.

That was the last time I spoke with Agnes. She died while I was away. I was so grateful that I had listened to my internal voice and in doing so I had been given the gift of our last conversation.

From my perspective, it hadn't been her time to die years earlier. It seems these years had been a piece of her life journey that she was meant to live. And when it was her time, an unexpected thing happened. Agnes had not been feeling well, so she had gone to the cancer center. She died there that day from an overdose of radiation. It was not the cancer that had killed her.

Part of the story around cancer is that it will kill you. "*Incurable.*" Sometimes it does, and sometimes it doesn't, but it's the story that it *does* or *will* kill you that is the point. In reality, we don't know what is going to result from the disease and, generally, we become blind to the possibility of the gift in the disease.

I was in a workshop with a woman, a physician. Her story, as she told it there, was so powerful that it has remained with me all these years. She and her husband were a couple without children, purposefully so because they were so bonded to each other that they literally did not want to share the other with a child. They worked together in medical research while she also had a practice. They were making love one day when he found a lump on her breast. She explained how she had checked it out for herself and was convinced, given its particular characteristics, that it was benign. His reaction was somewhat harsh: "You're having a biopsy first thing in the morning," and no amount of protest from her was going to change that.

The immediate results showed cancer that had spread into the lymphatic system. She underwent surgery, yet both of them felt she would not survive long, given the lymph contamination. Although neither had had a spiritual practice up to this point, they set about preparing for her death. This included doing a number of workshops along with voracious reading.

Then they went skiing one day and the husband was killed instantly in a "freak" accident. He was coming down a run with a curving path and ran head on into a snow-grooming machine that *wasn't supposed to be there*. She, on the other hand, is still alive and doing very well, twenty-odd years later.

The cancer? It appears to no longer be there and, no, she did not have any conventional treatment following her husband's death. Although it would be foolhardy and false to even attempt to explain this odd twist of events, it would seem that her husband's life story included his dying at that time, while her cancer, in provoking awareness of the bigger picture through their mutual spiritual exploration, was a necessary part of each of their journeys. Agnes during her last six and a half years expanded within herself. I can easily imagine the same for this husband and wife—it seems that her cancer served both of them.

We make up stories about everything in life. Anything that is not of this moment includes mind-memory and story. Some stories are just told and that's the end of it. Others, however, the ones of interest for our self-growth investigation, are those we hang on to and use to keep our internal fires going. Oddly enough, these held-on-to stories give us the illusion of excitement or perhaps worthiness to our life. They become a way for us to be identified. We do this around all our relationships—our lovers, family, and friends—and our health. We make up stories of how certain outcomes are inevitable, just because of our beliefs associated with the subject. Life does show us otherwise, yet often we chose not to notice.

Stories have the effect of helping us to hold onto the energy because we get to repeat them over and over and over again. In some cases, people are aware of their story as a story and they may also be aware that they want to hold on to them. Most of the time, however, people are unconscious of their desire to not let go. In many ways, held-on-to stories become part of our identification, an identification that we are involved with and attached to. The notion of unfairness in life could be an example, or of how you didn't do anything to deserve this kind of treatment. There's juice in holding on. Usually when we see someone who is using a story over and over, it is serving the person by getting them attention. It draws people to them in sympathy or in trying to make them feel better.

We have stored-up stories that we often repeat or, on the contrary, stuff away, as Henry did. Resentments, regrets, and held-on-to stories are huge wastes of our energy. They weigh on us, they hold us down, they tire us. Some illnesses such as fibromyalgia will, in energetic medicine, have links to these old energies.

We construct our own stories according to our filters. For example, if someone hasn't been in touch with you and you have issues around feeling left out, then you will likely create a story that drops you into feeling not good enough or not being likable. How many stories are in your life that have absolutely nothing to do with today? Often these are about held-on-to regrets (what if I had done things differently?) or resentments (toward someone or something). To really get mileage, the story will be repeated to each friend, one by one. The more it is repeated, the more imbedded it becomes. Even though we are all aware that the past is the past and it cannot be changed, we will still hash something over and over as though the past is about this moment. "My mother always told me I was supposed to be nice, because everyone likes nice people," is, for example, part of a story that includes more detail. The question is, who are you today? Are you still the little girl being conditioned to behave in a particular way so as to please your mother? Knowing this piece of yourself, of course, is helpful to your self-understanding; it's the hanging on to it, having the past impact your response to life today, that is the burden.

In the humor of the Universe, while I was writing this chapter I also created a drama story of my own which went on quite a few days before I was jolted into seeing it for what it was. I hadn't heard from someone, a person I care about who generally stays in touch, for some time. An email from me had not produced a response. My mind then started creating one scenario of explanations after another until I was truly caught in the involved drama of my own making. The jolt back to reality came when I phoned this person and found out that indeed he had been in touch through email but I had not received it. To satisfy me further, he read me the note on the phone and then sent it to me so I couldn't continue with my involvement by saying, "he just said he had written when he hadn't." Only once I was faced with this reality check was I able to see how unconscious I had been. The Universe had provided me with an opportunity and I had had a short-term failure. To be clear, it's not that we stop, for example, creating stories as an illusion of feeling in control of life. Rather, as we focus our attention more on increasing our awareness, what shifts is our ability to catch our involvement more quickly. Sometimes, for me, I can have almost immediate awareness, although still in the past tense after the fact, or it can take a bit of time, as was the case with the above story.

Again, it's the involvement that turns the story from just a story into pathology. I used to know some of the biggest-named reporters in the world and from them I learned just how much our news of the world is manipulated. In today's world, it is even more pronounced because of the control of the media having been reduced now to only a few powerful men. Yet we turn on our TV, watch the news, and believe that what we are being told is all true. We become attached and involved and we debate points with our friends, further embedding the given facts as reality.

There are also the stories that are held onto when someone dies. You see this more clearly in countries or among cultures where the women wear something that indicates they have lost their husband. This may mean wearing black, for example, to denote their widowhood, or having a traditional facial marking removed, such as a bindi in India, to identify them. These visible (or now invisible) markings invite a repeat of the story of the person who died, while attempting to keep the deceased alive, in memory. In another form of this, we often see where stories of a loved one, be it a partner or a parent or even a close friend, get repeated as a part of a person's identification. So very often, when a person is open enough to look at this honestly, they will see that the story is actually an attempt to keep the deceased person alive. Underlying the repeating of the stories there is usually guilt around the fading memory of the loved one. A wanting to hang on.

Yet what do you get from holding on to the story? What difference does it honestly make what someone said or what someone did? What keeps you from simply saying, "Well, that's an interesting perspective" and leaving it at that? The difference in the story being pathological for us lies in the involvement. The story itself becomes a part of our identification of who we think we are rather than simply being a part of the life we've lived. It is when we are attached—and we know we are attached, when we continuously repeat the same story—that the pathology comes into play.

My brother held a grudge against me for years. As it is with all stories, the details don't matter, but I had said something to him that included money and our dad. Issues of money in families are almost always triggers, plus, in my brother's case, his left-wanting relationship with our dad, contrary to the catering-to that I received, provided the fuel. Like the cap off the toothpaste, he held on to his angry resentment for years.

The above story is true. But now I'll combine some of what was true with some fictional pieces, in order to illustrate why I said that holding on to old tapes and resentments is a huge waste of energy. Let's say my brother hadn't seen me for quite some time, and he saw me only when "forced" to through some family function because he didn't want to upset our mother. During one of these functions, I engaged him, just asking how he was, genuinely seeking communication. For me, I had years ago let go of any energy around that past event. That doesn't mean I didn't remember it if, for whatever reason, it popped into my mind, but I did not have a charge around it. There was some memory and that's all. But my brother definitely still had a charge. He was seething inside over this one event, it was obvious to see, and I imagine he was running the tape over and over again in his mind, repeating what I had said so long ago and ending by declaring what a liar I am.

Whenever we are holding on to something, making it someone else's fault, it takes energy. Continuing with this imagined story, let's say that as soon as he was able to leave after the family function, and starting with the ride home in the car, he started repeating the story, now out loud, to his wife and anyone else around. You can almost feel the energy building, can't you?

Now let's move to the next morning. Using the analogy of money, suppose we can say that we all wake up from our night's sleep with $100 worth of energy. Continuing with this illustration, let's just suppose for the story sake that my brother, having held on to his anger and resentment from the night before, lies in bed with his wife and starts in all over again, repeating the old story while adding in about how I said such-and-such the night before, and then I did this and that, and he really hadn't wanted to talk to me in the first place! By the time he gets out of bed, holding on to this past event and his anger toward me, he has used up let's say $35 worth of energy. He gets into the shower, now yelling so his wife can hear him, "And this isn't the only time she acted like this. I remember when we were..." and away he goes, spewing out more held-on-to energy. There goes another $25 worth of energy. "And you could have said something to her, you know," he yells, accusing his wife for not having taken "his side," and there goes another $10 of energy.

Before he has even left the bathroom, much less had breakfast, he has already spent a whopping $70 of his day's $100 worth of energy. Want to look at where fatigue and body pain comes from? This could be a good start.

In the Judeo-Christian perspective, forgiveness is often interpreted as saying something like, "I know you didn't mean to do what you did, and I want you to know I'm a big enough person to be able to say I forgive you for what you did to me." Really? Do you think that's what is meant by forgiveness? Try this perspective on and see if you can relate to it. The act need not be forgiven; forgiveness is given to the person in recognition of their humanness, with the understanding that we have not been perfect in our own lives. We know nothing about another person's life nor what the filters were that drove them to the act. Christ said, "He that is without sin among you, let him first cast a stone at her." (John 8:7) Isn't Christ saying we cannot judge another? To use a well-known metaphor, when we judge someone, we are pointing our finger at them and there are then three pointing fingers coming back to ourselves; in other words, whenever we feel the need to judge another, we are judging ourselves. Might forgiveness actually be toward ourselves for our inability to let go of our resentment? Might forgiveness be in the opening of our heart? I remember a moment of saying, "Thank you, God, that I do not have to live my life as Saddam Hussein. I imagine he has a very painful life."

According to all ancient texts—and, yes, that does include those from the Judeo-Christian perspective—the path to knowing God is through one's self. Going back to the example of my brother, let's imagine that the mere sight of me or even the mention of my name or perhaps just something that to anyone else would be meaningless might somehow have been a reminder to him of his unresolved feelings about me. I was the object outside of him that stirred his internal pot and, because he was not going to explore himself, he projected his feelings out on me. He had a reaction to me, the object, which in turn brought up the long-since told story and the re-play of the very old tape. There was no way in his mind that he was going to forgive me. What I had said was unforgivable and the only resolution would come with my saying: "I'm sorry, I didn't mean to say that and I know it was not true." No matter what it cost him, I imagine he held on to it until his death, though perhaps with a bit less charge. In holding on to our past, reliving it through our stories, and being unwilling to forgive what life presents us with, we lose the opportunity to be with this moment.

Now, what if, just what if, the perspective shifted from "Me" being the person for you to blame to "me" being a gift from God? Flipping this around will change your life, I promise you. Every time there is an object outside of yourself that pushes your buttons or, as I am known for saying, "stirs your internal pot to bubbling," shifting your perspective from blame to seeing it as a gift is powerful. In this way, the person or object has given you a perfect opportunity to honestly drop into what you're feeling, under all of the projection—an opportunity to explore what is lying in your underbelly. Now you'll have your $100 worth of energy to use throughout your day in fulfilling ways.

If you are holding on to anything, anything at all that is not of this moment, not right now, acknowledge that and move on. What is past truly, literally, is past. Over. Done with. The need to make it someone else's fault that it unfolded as it did is one of the most futile wastes of energy you could have. My interpretation comes from my perception; my brother's came from his. He could not possibly know what was going on for me at the time I said what I did, nor could I of him. *Why did I* bring this up at that time when I hadn't said anything for years? I imagine it's because I was holding on to some energy around this event even though I wasn't consciously aware of doing so. In expressing what I needed to say to my brother, and then going deeper with my feelings around the event, I released it for me, whereas for him, it seems, the story just kept being repeated.

How many relationship stories have you heard? This area is where we see so many, and usually they are related to something one of the partners did that was not acceptable to the other. I created a story all around blame pointed at my last husband so that I didn't have to look at my own participation in the relationship. Far easier to blame him than to look at the dark pieces of me that were fighting their way to the surface of my consciousness. There is a lot of juice in holding on to how one person harmed the other. "You hurt me." "You betrayed my trust." "How could you do this to me?" "You can't love me if you had an affair." These are sufficiently common to use as examples, regardless of who speaks them. Yet they are all charged statements—they all have hooks embedded in them in that they are attempts to control the other person through guilt, plus they are all based on the person's beliefs. Here's a pretty simple question: Who is the one person you can trust? If you feel hurt, who is responsible for the hurt? Try "Mirror, mirror on the wall." Most people don't like to hear it when I say that no one can hurt you, and immediately the stories come spewing out of their mouths in protest. But no matter what, the reason you feel hurt is not because the external person/object—in this example, the unfaithful partner—hurt you, but because of what got stirred in you, deep in those caves, by the held-on-to beliefs around your relationship to yourself as well as, let's say in this case, to men.

Upon introspection it might be that someone just cannot get past what is perceived as betrayal. Although it should be simple enough to say, "This is unacceptable to me," and then act from that place, alas, I have rarely seen it unfold in that manner. Instead, it tends to manifest in an ugly way with a lot of projection, blame, and guilt. In all fairness, there's no question that betrayal is a loaded dynamic for most people, with many layers. In my experience, betrayal is probably the most difficult dynamic to work through. But does that mean you want to submerge your feelings, stuff them away into dark corners? Remember the saying, "What you resist persists." Submerged pieces have their own sneaky way of coming up and slapping you in another way—usually, in this case, in your next relationship.

Many people have secrets, and if there is a secret, there will be a story to cover it. Actually, the secret itself is also a story. I have already shared some of mine, so I know from my own experience what happens when the secret is brought out of the closet into the conscious state. The crazy thing is that we live in fear of revealing our secrets for fear of the risk while, in reality, bringing a secret forward and revealing it is freeing.

One of the most dramatic secrets I know of belonged to my mother, one she held on to for sixty-three years, never daring to tell anyone. She shared her secret only with her favorite sister, so that it wasn't entirely submerged, but once the sister died, it became deeply buried again. When the events unfolded that brought this piece of the past to my mother's conscious surface, and once she told me, there was a palpable sense of relief for her as well as a physical sensation of relief. "I feel like this huge weight has been lifted from me. It's been such a burden to keep it to myself," was how she described it.

Although I have gone to great lengths to avoid identification of the characters in this book, in the following story, because of life circumstances of the main character having been dramatically altered and in honor of the participants, I am using their actual names. This is a fantastic true story that illustrates some real-life gems, including, as we see yet again, how the mystery of life truly does unfold in spite of us, with grace, and how the story that was held on to for so many years had nothing to do with what had actually happened.

There are many old sayings that have been passed on about family ties, such as, "Blood is thicker than water." Family bonds are born of patterns that are formed from the beliefs within the immediate family, the extended family, and the ancestral material. The latter, the ancestral material, is incredibly significant in its impact on current patterns someone may be expressing. Further, we like to think we're original and that "We" decided to do a particular thing or take a certain decision. Yet see how you feel about all this after you have read the following story.

My mother, Jessie, called me one December 22nd. "Sit down, please, I have a story I need to tell you. I've just had a phone call from a woman and I want you to know what she called about. Your aunt Francis (my mother's youngest sister), was 15 when she went to work, after school, for a widower with two teenage boys. She was wanting to make some money so she could buy herself some new clothes. That all changed when one of them (I don't remember if it was the father or one of the boys) raped her and she became pregnant. Only my mother and I ever knew about this [out of the family of then eight children]. Your brother was a baby then, and I had asked my dad if Francis could come to live with us because I was also running our business and could use her help. In this way, not even my dad ever found out about the pregnancy. When my sister Francis' baby was born, my mother and I immediately took her across the street to the Salvation Army for adoption. This woman who just called is saying she is that baby. She says her name is Maxine."

From there the story unfolded in a most amazing way. Just after the New Year, my mother and I flew to the city where Maxine lives, to meet her. My elderly mother, in all fairness, kept questioning whether or not the woman could possibly be who she said she was. "How could she have found me?" was a question my mother repeated several times. My mother was the only surviving member of her family. My aunt Francis had gone on to later marry Ron and they had two children—a boy, Don, and a girl, Carol. The family pattern there was so strong that Francis died at age 50 and her son Don also died at age 50, both from illness. The daughter Carol (the one from the swan story in the Dark-Shaman chapter) died in her sleep at age 50. So there was no one related to this story who was alive except for my mother.

My mother was feeling increasingly nervous and emotional as we got closer to meeting her unknown niece in the airport. So, after finding my mother a place to sit down, I went to fetch our luggage. I immediately noticed the back of a woman, went up to her, and addressed her by name. She spun around while asking incredulously, "How did you know it was me?" "Because you are just like your mother." I said this because of her physical appearance—her body shape, her body language—and, as you will see, the patterns went far deeper than the physical.

My now newly discovered cousin Maxine looked the way her mother had looked before she died. Although the hair color of what I'll call "mousey brown," which is not quite grey, was the same, it was the sameness of the hairstyle that first struck me. Her mother Francis had always permed her hair. I even remember my mother doing it for her, and here, more than sixty years later, was this woman with the exact same permed hairstyle.

As we were pulling out of the airport, a song came on the radio—Bette Midler singing "The Rose." By then I was really feeling into the wonder of this experience as I said, "This was your sister Carol's favorite song. It was played at her funeral and it's what her son played at his wedding." Obviously shaken, my cousin said, "It's my favorite song and my youngest son played it at his wedding."

Entering her home, it was amusing to me to see how much it felt like her mother's home. Memories of my aunt Francis had become like a movie running in front of me, all verified by my bewildered, overwhelmed mother, as I remembered details long forgotten. One of these that popped into my mind ever so clearly was how my aunt had set days of the week for individual chores: one day was for laundry, one was for cleaning, and so on. I was to learn later during our visit how not only did my cousin do the same, but she even had the same chores on the same days as her mother had had.

Sitting us in her kitchen, my cousin Maxine made tea served with cookies, just as her mother had, served in the exact same china pattern of tea cup and from the exact same style tea pot of the same pattern with the exact same small plates for the cookies. Imagine! Besides the cups, teapot, and dessert plates, Maxine's everyday dishes turned out to also be the same pattern as those that Francis, her mother, had used. And if you think that's not enough, at dinner we were served on the same pattern dishes as my grandmother, her grandmother, had had.

When I was growing up, Sunday dinner was just something you had to go to, and to say you didn't want to go was met with a tush-tush and disapproving glares, so you went rather than put up with a guilt trip. One Sunday my mother would have the dinner, the next the aunt of this story would, and on the third Sunday another aunt had it. My mother was a great cook, so she would vary her dinners somewhat, but my aunt of this story always cooked the exact same meal every time it was her turn. With great amusement, I watched as my cousin prepared her dinner. As her mother had done, she had everything pre-cut, waiting in order, to be cooked. Of course, by now, you've guessed that my cousin cooked the exact same dinner down to a tee, including the pickles and dessert.

I had noticed by this point Maxine's same crooked index finger, like her mother's. Later I would see the same handwriting that brought instant recall of my aunt's letters to me years before. To top off these same-nesses, my aunt Francis had her favorite perfume that, I had thought at the time, would have long since been discontinued, but nope, here was her daughter wearing the same perfume.

Now here's the really fascinating, and not to be denied magic, of the unfolding of this particular story, full of gifts for anyone reading it. First, though, a little reminder of how the famous Swiss psychiatrist Carl Jung coined the phrase "The Shadow" to refer to the unconscious. The Shadow, as we all know, is elusive and we don't see our own. Later, others began using "The Dark Side" as an alternative way to describe that which we keep hidden in our unconscious. For example, everything I ever denied about my mother was in me, even though I suppressed it, kept it hidden, because I did not want to have to embrace these unwanted pieces of myself.

Now to this cousin's story. Maxine had been adopted by a family from a city a few hundred miles from here, and later they moved to the city where we visited her. In her mid-teens she met Jack, the man who would become her husband in a couple of years. He would often say to her, "Why don't you try and find your mother Maxine? You'll find it's not the story you think it is," to which Maxine would angrily lash back with: "I have no interest in finding her. She didn't want me and I don't want her."

One day Jack dropped dead in the kitchen. But she remembered her husband's words.

After two or three years, a friend said, "I think it's time you have a vacation, and we should go golfing for a few weeks," so away they went. Now it *just so happened* that they booked at a motel called The Shadow Inn. How much more fun does it get than that? The Shadow Inn! The Universe does have humor in its perfection. A few days later, Maxine and her friend were paired up for their golf foursome with an elderly couple from my city, Don and Jean. During the game, the elderly man kept asking her questions such as, "Where were you born?" and "Did you ever find out who your mother is?"

Later, while they were all having a drink, Don dropped the bombshell. "I know who your mother was. I'm pretty sure it was so-and-so," naming my aunt Francis. "But, if not, it was her sister Jessie," meaning my mother. "Jean and I were best friends with Francis and her husband Ron. Your mother's gone now, but I'm going to give you the phone number of her husband. You need to find this out. Call him." As with my own experience, he could say this with such conviction because his experience of Maxine left no doubt for him about who she was.

It was still a struggle for Maxine, however, as she repeated in her mind that her mother had not wanted her and had abandoned her. But the window had been opened and there was no turning back. First came contacting the government to obtain whatever minimal information they had. As it turned out, the vital piece was my aunt's last name, although no other information was available. Gathering her courage, she phoned Francis' husband Ron. Upon hearing that his wife's last name was that on Maxine's birth certificate, there was no longer a question. Now Maxine knew who her mother was. After hearing her story, my uncle Ron said, "I always knew Francis had a secret." He then told her my mother Jessie would be the only one who would know anything and added, "If Jessie's the one who's been keeping the secret all these years, I doubt she'll tell you." She then called my mother, and the rest you already know.

When my mother and I had visited a few months earlier, my mother had given her niece Maxine a photo of her mother Francis, in a sterling silver frame, which Maxine gave a place of honor on a table in her living room. Several months later, my uncle Ron wanted to meet Maxine, this daughter of his late wife Francis, and her family. Maxine's one son who had had "The Rose" played at his wedding, had a daughter 18 months old, who, along with her parents, was there for the dinner.

When my uncle Ron arrived, he was so struck by Maxine's appearance that he burst into tears at the remembered familiarity of his long-since deceased wife.

While my cousin's whole family was gathered in the kitchen, having tea, the well-mannered little granddaughter uncharacteristically toddled off into the living room. Although she would never normally touch anything, she picked up the silver-framed photo of her great grandmother, waddled back into the kitchen, and placed it in my uncle Ron's lap. Oh, and just to finish off this story filled with grace, the middle name of Maxine's granddaughter is Rose, the same as that of her great grandmother Francis!

What a multitude of forces had to come together for this scene to be enacted! What perfection created by the Universe! Regardless of one's perspective, one has to willingly acknowledge that the key actor, my cousin Maxine, was not in charge of the unfolding of these events. Life didn't care whether or not she wanted to discover her mother. When it was time to unveil this piece, it was time. Finding the story very different from the one she had told herself all these years changed her life, including giving her great peace. There was no need to even think of forgiveness—it was just there. For my mother, it relieved her of the heavy burden of having held on to this secret for so many years and also gave her inner peace.

In this beautiful, succinct quote, Nelson Mandela describes the energy of holding on to stories that no longer serve. "As I walked out the door toward my freedom, I knew if I did not leave all the anger, hatred, and bitterness behind that I would still be in prison."

And so it is when we refuse to forgive, when we blame God or when we insist on blaming the other person. Indeed, we often blame life itself because it hasn't been what it was supposed to have been.

Like everything else about ourselves, it's not about self-judgment. Rather, just become aware and notice when you bring forward a story, one that has been repeated many times, that has nothing to do with the moment you are experiencing. That's the clue. When you have a button pushed, if you go a bit deeper, your body will give you a clue and you will likely notice contractions or some other bodily sensation as you once again relive the story. The sensation may even be excitement because the story makes you feel alive. Just the conscious awareness that you are repeating a story from the past helps to dissolve its usefulness. The memory will stay, but the shift will have only taken away the charge you have been getting from re-telling the story. Releasing the story is another piece toward freedom.

CHAPTER NINE:

All the Things We Don't Want in Our Lives

Honesty is the capacity for presence, and the ability and willingness to simply describe things as they are. Idealism and anti-idealism become positions of the mind. They become a way of seducing yourself back into attachment, to beliefs about how things should be rather than being present to what is.

Brad Blanton

Someone who had been very special and meaningful to me came back into my life a little while ago. Yes, wonderful and totally unforeseen. Over time, he slowly told me the story of how, having found the love of his life and married her, he had shared with his wife a profound connection and the sacred intimacy that comes from a relationship on that level. After too few years of sharing such space, she became ill. He stuck by her side, caring for her himself throughout her long illness until she died. My heart hurt for him as I heard his story. The tragedy of soul-love found and lost.

We witness much in our world today that gives us cause to feel despair, sadness, and anger. We hear of someone's young granddaughter having been raped; we hear of the senseless shooting of a teen by police; we hear of a train driver who suddenly drives his train at high speeds and crashes, killing a hundred passengers. It's not only the person who was directly impacted by an event who feels the pain, it spreads to everyone in that person's life and fans out from there.

These are not events we want in our life, yet the pain and the suffering open hearts. We humans would rather avoid discomfort and certainly pain, or anything that speaks to us in a heart-wrenching way, in whatever way we can. We often resort to extraordinary measures to avoid pain. Addictions—and please don't think you don't have any—are good stuffing tools to hide away the pain: sex, sugar, food, alcohol, cosmetic alterations, cigarettes, prescription drugs (we kid ourselves by saying they aren't really drugs because a doctor prescribed them), shopping, gambling, T.V., and anything else that can keep our feelings in check. And then life gives us such a whammy that we are torn apart. *Then* we feel.

Pain—when fully experienced—*will* shift and morph into a sense of calm, ease, inner peace, and even joy. It's when we stuff away whatever is arising in us that we experience that which is contrary to our natural state of Beingness. When I was spending a lot of time in Africa, I learned how Africans respond when someone they love dies. The apartment I was renting had an African caretaker for the building. One day I saw him leaving with a little bag. He didn't check with the administrator to ask if his leaving was all right. He was suddenly leaving because, as he told me, someone he cared about had died. There was no question for him, even though he was a poor man and it was a considerable cost for him to travel the great distance by bus. Africans gather to grieve the loss of someone in their lives. They fully grieve. They cry, they moan, they scream, they dance, they talk, and they don't stop for several days. They don't try to run away from their pain, rather they experience their pain completely. And when the grieving is complete, they move on with their lives. They have had closure.

So often in our world, grief, like other emotions, is suppressed because we see it as something to be avoided—we want to avoid the suffering of loss because it is just way too painful. As with the woman who had the collapsed lung when her ideal marriage collapsed, when an emotion or energy is suppressed, it gets stored somewhere in the body and, eventually, there will be some physical manifestation.

We also seem to have a need to continue to ask "Why?" or "How could this have happened?" Yet when we sit with whatever is in front of us, there is no questioning. It simply is.

The freedom comes when we are able to experience whatever emotion or energy an event has stirred in us, to sit fully and completely in our grief, for example, or our anger. It is only through this experience that there can be a release. The understanding that life unfolds as it will, without participation from you, adds to the freedom. The more you experience the truth of this, the more it will be your truth.

What has happened, has happened. It cannot be taken back. Even though the mind tortures us by saying it could have been prevented, and tries to prove it with a story of "if only," it did happen. Freedom comes in being okay with life as it is: the such-ness or is-ness of life, as my teacher Brugh Joy used to say.

We all know this, and it's been known for eons. So what is it in us that has us in a state of forgetting? Why do we notice the feeling and then stuff it, so we get caught again in the illusion that we have anything to do with what life presents us?

As I see it, the out-of-the-ordinary happens in an attempt to wake us up. It's as though we are getting a profound message, "Look, look, do you think you could stop this unfolding? If you think you could, tell me how you would do that." This is the whole point of "*and it just so happened.*"

There was a young African man who had gone to study in a small city. One day he was walking a quiet street, listening to some music through his headphones. Imagine him as he was boppin' along, moving to the music. A little farther down the street some people were walking toward this young man. Nearby, a helicopter was flying with three men in it—the pilot and two environmental researchers. Something happened to the helicopter and the pilot was unable to control it. The pedestrians were able to see this struggling, rapidly descending helicopter, but the African, focused on his music, knew nothing of it. The other people on the street were all screaming at him, but he couldn't hear. The helicopter came crashing down on him, and all four men were instantly killed. (CBC News, Cranbrook, BC, Canada, May 2008)

Can your mind conjure a more bizarre event than this? Imagine his family in Africa. Do you think they would believe such a story? If they were from a small village, let's say, it is likely they may never have even seen a helicopter, so this event would be incomprehensible. What might their own version of the story be? He was murdered and the government is trying to cover up the truth.

A family of four was driving on a two-lane highway. The father was driving, the mother was in the passenger seat, and the children were in the back. An eighteen-wheeler truck came by them, going in the opposite direction, and a large rock was thrown up from one of its tires. The rock went through the windshield and hit the mother in the head, killing her instantly. (CBC News, Western Canada, 2012)

Two young boys, aged five and seven, went to spend the night at their friend's home on an island off eastern Canada. The father of their friend owned a pet store and the family lived above it. During the night, a five-foot python escaped from its cage, even though it had been in the same cage without incident for over thirteen years, and made its way through the ducting to the upstairs. It killed both boys, suffocating them in their sleep. A friend of mine who grew up on a game reserve in Africa, and who knows a tremendous amount about animals and reptiles, says this is completely out of character for the snake. If it had been hungry, which was not the case, it would have killed only one boy. So why both young boys, without any attempt to eat them? (CBC News, NBC News, New Brunswick, Canada, August 2013)

And just in case you're still not convinced, here's another dramatic story. A woman borrowed her sister's BMW to take her 10-year-old and 10-month-old daughters away for a short trip. Although the older girl had wanted to sit in the front seat, the mother had her sit in the back. The infant was in a car seat, behind the mother's seat, facing backwards. The car was rear-ended by a truck, which sent the car into a spin on the bridge they *just happened to be on*. The car ended up dangling over the edge of the bridge. The truck, also out of control, plunged over the bridge, and burst into flames as it landed in the deep ravine below, killing the driver.

Now it *just so happened* that the car was hanging on the railing on the side of the freeway going in the opposite direction. Firefighters were quick on the scene and began a desperate attempt to free the terrified mother and her children. However, every time they tried to reach the children, the car slid a bit further. Understandably, once the fire trucks arrived, traffic in both directions was stopped, as drivers watched what was happening. Now it *just so happened* there were some Navy Seabee construction workers, who had been delayed and therefore were behind the rest of their corps, causing them to be caught in the traffic of this accident. A couple of the Seabees walked the highway to get to the scene of the accident, where they were able to see immediately the severity of the problem that the firefighters were facing, with the car slipping bit by bit over the bridge. And, according to some bigger plan, it *just so happened* that the Seabees had a large forklift they were transporting. They were on the opposite side of the freeway, so they were able to stabilize the dangling car by placing the forklift under it, which allowed the firefighters to work more vigorously in freeing the family. As well, it *just so happened* that the baby slept through the entire drama and therefore didn't rock the car. The mother and her older daughter suffered only minor injuries, while the baby was uninjured. (NBC News, February 2013)

Mind-boggling yet, as part of our human nature, we have a tendency to attempt to explain unusual happenings by phrases such as "a freak accident" or asking repeatedly, "How could this happen?" because we want an explanation. We want to know why. If we have an answer to "why," then we have the illusion of feeling safer. Yet the unfolding, even including the role of other people in the events, simply happened. What does it take to drop us into the realization of how life unfolds? I mentioned at the beginning of this book that looking back on your own life will show you undeniably the magic of this unfolding and how, although you may have thought at the time that you had some say in what appeared in your life, it really wasn't true.

In writing up these examples, I am struck over and over by the Mystery of Life—that which is unexplainable to the mind yet cracks open the heart a tiny bit more. Although we may not want our painful experiences, we are nevertheless powerless in their unfolding, bringing us to the place of knowing that we cannot know why. Yet, bit by bit, we learn to trust that it is a part of our script, simply because we had the experience. It doesn't take away the pain. What it does do is put the event in perspective through the realization that we have no way of knowing the "why" or the bigger plan.

A young family I knew moved to England for the father's work. They were excited to be there, as it was advancement for the father in his work and a great international experience for the children. Everyone was learning English as well as how to find their way around London, a city that was still foreign to them.

When people move to England, probably one of their first purchases is an umbrella, because we all know the country has a reputation for rain. One day the mother took her two youngest children shopping. The youngest, a four-year-old boy, was super excited because they bought an umbrella. The children and the mother, holding each child's hand, were stopped at a traffic light. This little four-year-old, ecstatic over having an umbrella, hit the release button just as a car came whizzing by. The car caught the umbrella; the boy was thrown under the car and killed instantly. The tragic heartbreak for this young family, the sense of despair and helplessness that could be felt by those who knew them, was indescribable. What can you possibly say in such a situation? There is nothing consolable; the pain is too unbearable and must be endured.

The mystery of pain and death of a young child showing up this way is truly heart-wrenching. Still, is there any way for anyone to deny the unfolding that simply happened, without any participation from anyone else? What does it take to drop us into the realization of this? As I have just mentioned again, looking back on your own life will show you undeniably the magic of this unfolding, regardless of whether we wanted the particular unfolding or not.

When we make a decision or a plan, we feel totally in charge, or at least we want to think we are. Yet we know from experiments showing the time-delay between an event and the brain processing the information that everything we are experiencing is already in the past tense, so should we then be taking credit for our wise decision? Even though it is only a fraction of a second before "we" have any cognition of the act we are experiencing, is half a second any different from ten years? Isn't the past, the past? If we know this, how is it that we still get caught in thinking we made a "wrong" decision?

A friend and I went out for lunch one birthday of mine, during which we were talking about areas of the city we wanted to live in. Later, as I was driving her home, we passed an old farmhouse on a beautiful little lot that had been there for the better part of a hundred years. I wistfully said to my friend, "Now *this* is where I would like to live!" As I heard myself say that, I stopped the car. The owner was in his garden and I went over to talk to him. I told him how I remembered this house from my childhood and how I had always liked it. Somewhere in the conversation, I gave him my name, to which he responded by asking the name of my dad. It *just so happened* that he had done work for my dad many years before and was an admirer of his. "Please give me a call if ever you decide to sell your place," said I, to which he replied, "Well it *just so happens* my wife and I were talking about that this very morning because we would like to move to a small town." We agreed on a price then and there. We shook hands on the deal just, as he said, "like your dad always did, and I knew I could trust him."

The land purchase was a true coup, given to me by Grace. After acquiring the adjacent property, I went on to do a condominium project. However, as I was out of funds from purchasing the land, I joined in a co-venture partnership with a builder. Although I did my homework by carefully checking the builder's work (all of which had been individually custom-built to that point) as well as having tight legal documents drawn up and signed to prevent any difficulty, I neverthe-less was cheated out of earning the profit I had anticipated from this successful venture. The builder walked away with my share and his. From my legal inves-tigation that followed, I learned I would undoubtedly win the case. There were several catches to taking it to court, however: it would take considerable time, perhaps a couple of years, and it would cost a large sum of money—ironically, about what I would have earned on the project—and by the time it actually went to court, the builder would have moved all his assets, so there would be nothing for me to gain. The net result would be that I would have lost money on the case, money I simply didn't have, just to show I had been cheated. Well-written contracts are simply a stated intention, not a guarantee. So what had started out with such excitement ended up being a very unpleasant and certainly unwanted event. It was also a huge turning point in my life that ultimately ended up in my having to work in order to survive. And, of course, as Grace was in charge, the next phase of my life began to unfold.

Faced with the seriousness of my financial situation, I knew I needed to start working. After having talked with the local medical school and being told I could attend, I was about to return to my medical studies as an advanced-aged student. I began studying and refreshing my knowledge. It was during this time that a friend phoned and invited me to attend a lecture on a new modality in energy medicine. Although she was extremely excited about this, my answer was firm. I was absolutely not interested in learning yet another modality. My friend insisted and, at some point, I observed my resistance and gave in. "All right, I'll go. I do need to know what's out there."

As I listened to the founder of this energy healing system (The BodyTalk System) speak, I found all my resistance melting away and excitement taking its place. What he was saying made such sense to me. Indeed, my desire on finishing medical school was to be doing just what he was talking about, using my background but linking it to energy medicine. My internal question quickly became one of, "So why am I going to go through the brutal program of medicine, internship, and residency at my age, when this is really what I would want to end up doing anyway?"

Hence, this next phase of my life began, and after some much briefer training in this energy medicine system than it would have been in conventional medicine, I was earning an income from something I loved doing by working as a practitioner plus teaching this system worldwide and training instructors. So, although my building project experience had been devastating, it was what pushed me into the place of finding a fulfilling and successful career. *Thanks be to Grace.*

Our beliefs have set up our ideal lives for us. We have said to God, "This is what I want," and "This is what I don't want," as though God cares. If we just look at the wonder of it all, we can see that we cannot be in charge of our lives, or those of others, or in charge of the world. We want to think we are in charge because there is such fear in letting go of our illusion of being in charge. We can, for example, practice a strong natural responsibility as a parent in providing the basic needs for our children: food, shelter, clothing, care, attention, and guidance. But we cannot protect them from their life's unfolding. The young mother I just mentioned was a very responsible, loving, and devoted mother. She was protectively holding her children's hands at the crosswalk, making sure they were safe when crossing the street. How could she have possibly anticipated her son pushing the release button on that umbrella just as the car came racing by? How could that young African man walking down the street, listening to his music, have prevented a helicopter from falling on him?

Once we honestly begin to examine life—not from the "love, light, and harmony" place, but from all that life is—a sense of peace descends. That doesn't mean we won't get caught in some beliefs and create suffering for ourselves, but it does mean we will suffer less. Experiencing the experience, being fully in the experience, feeling the pain, the joy, the anger, the fear, is what living a complete human life is. From being okay with life as it is, pure freedom abounds.

CHAPTER TEN:

I Will Not Forgive You, No Matter What

Forgiveness is a mystical act not a reasonable one.

Caroline Myss

Try on this simple perspective. Look at your house or apartment building from the front. Now look at it from the back and then from above in an imaginary helicopter. Each view of your house is different, yet the house itself is the same. Seeing it from the front gives us one perspective, while seeing it from the back gives a totally different one, and seeing it from above gives us the whole view that was not possible from either the front or the back. This is analogous to how we each have our unique perceptions of the same event. We tend to think of identical twins, for example, as being identical in every way. Indeed there are some amazing stories of geographically separated twins having similar traits and characteristics. But in relation to memory, there are often major differences. Of course, many memories will be more or less the same, yet often that is not the case. One twin will recall an event in one way, while the other will say something like, "No, no. That's not what he said." Although the two persons involved, in this case, were born at the same time, and experienced the same home environment and everything that goes with that, their own beliefs formed from their experiences are unique to them. This has often been validated in my groups by a participant who happens to be an identical twin.

When we are deeply embroiled in our story of what someone did to us, we dig in our heels and there's no budging us from our point of view, like the person in chapter one who will not forgive the offender. Now let's just see if we can shift that perception.

Look at any outside object—be it a person who said something to you, an event that you directly experienced, or perhaps one you simply heard about on television, or whatever. The object isn't important other than to recognize it is something outside of yourself. Now close your eyes and tune in to your body. Notice any sensations you may be feeling, perhaps tightness in your shoulders, a slight vibration in your gut, the rising of your chest as you breathe in. These belong to you; these are internal, they are not outside of you.

If you have someone whom you feel harmed you in some way, see if you can picture them now in your mind's eye. Perhaps they said some things you felt were cruel, or perhaps you felt betrayed as they told you what they had done. Perhaps they shared something that you had kept hidden in your cave and did not want to acknowledge, triggering a reaction in you. If you have this type of charged memory in your body storage, see if you can really bring this event forward so that you are seeing the person. Perhaps you are even beginning to have some internal sensation. And even if that is not happening for you at this moment, given an opportunity for you to repeat your story of harm done, you will be able to notice your reaction and accompanying body sensation.

What happens when we have an external event—in this case a person— and experience a reaction such as: "I will not speak to the offender again and, if you do, you are being disloyal to me," we can call this a charge. It's an energetic charge and it gets stored in the body.

Now the question to ask yourself is: can anyone make you feel any way? Seriously. Can another person be responsible for your anger toward them? If you feel betrayed, why is it that you feel this way? Can my words make you feel sad?

I mentioned this in the chapter on the formation of beliefs, and it's worth mentioning again. We experience life either by responding to it—as in enjoying, receiving, and giving—or we react to it. When we react, that means an internal button has been pushed. If a button gets pushed, that indicates you have unresolved issues in relationship to what was said or done. You may recall I say to people to consider that when your button is pushed it is a gift from God. This is an invitation to know yourself more intimately by self-examining what is in the charge for you. Whenever your button is pushed, it is never ever about the other person. Whenever your button is pushed, you are being asked to self-examine because the external factor has stirred something in your internal pot that you have been unwilling to examine.

I understand that you may immediately want to argue this point, because when we are caught up in a reaction, on some level we seem to want to stay there. If we are charged about a person or incident, we are determined to be right, plus it can be easier and much more exciting to keep the story going than to shift our perspective.

I had a client who refused to forgive his abusive mother. She was this and she was that; she was horrible, she abused me, she's a liar, she's every name you can think of. Even though this client gained insights in other areas, we would go round and round with this piece of the mother. He strongly identified with the story, with his younger self in this role, and he refused to let go. In truth, he had learned that he always gets attention and sympathy from telling his story of "poor me." This put him on center stage, so why let go? From my perspective in working with him, as long as he chose to stay with this worn-out tape he would be energetically stuck, not allowing for further growth. We finally broke through when I broached the subject of what he gets from the story. After releasing his resistance to owning how useful this story was to him, he was able to be self-honest and to see just how well this had served him. It got him a lot of attention and people quickly felt sorry for him, so from that he felt fed. He also owned the control he maintained over his mother—"I won't forgive you, you horrid person you!"—and admitted as well that it was useful to him with his partner, again as control, pulling out the story when needed. You see the point?

Worth pondering is a quote from Catherine Ponder. "When you hold resentment toward another, you are bound to that person or condition by an emotional link that is stronger than steel. Forgiveness is the only way to dissolve that link and get free."

True forgiveness can come only when we can forgive ourselves. When we expand our vision so as to see our full humanness—in the spectrum from our traits that we like and find acceptable at one end, in balance with the other end where those traits we strive to keep hidden reside—we emerge with a compassion born of true forgiveness. We have all said and done things that we hold some regret over. There is not one among us who is flawless in how we have approached life and those we have shared it with.

For sure I have said things I wish I hadn't said. For sure I have wondered, "Where in the hell did that come from?" because it seemed out of character for me. That is until I am reminded that "out of character for me" simply means some denied piece of myself.

Jung would say that the dragon's tail will come up and slap you from behind if the shadow pieces are ignored, which means that the unclaimed pieces will come out in some fashion, whether we want them to or not. And, indeed, that's what happens. There can be no balance if one pole is grossly weighted while the other is weightless from not being claimed.

Turn your mind back to chapter two, where I tell of the situation in which one sister accused another sister of lying, thereby splintering the entire family dynamics. You may recall that the "victim" sister will not forgive the "offender" sister for what she said. The only way she will forgive, and that may not even prove to be true, is if the offender will take back every word she said about the event. Really? How is it anyone can take back that which has been said? The sister who feels offended is simply hanging on to a story that no longer serves her, and it certainly does not serve the family harmony. Every time the story is repeated, the distortion will get bigger and indeed, in doing so, it will burrow in ever deeper.

Yes, the offender sister did say some things that appear to have hurt the victim sister. Now, however, let's look at that from a bigger vision. First, we could say that no one, and that includes the offender sister herself, can say what made her say such things. When the unconscious strikes, when the tail of the dragon hits us, we see just how out of control we are in our perceived world of control. Second, the victim sister doesn't know a thing about what was going on in the life of her sister at the moment of this encounter, even though she maybe thinks she does. I could make up a story and list of all sorts of possibilities, any one of which could be true or not. So let's try on this one. Perhaps the offender sister was struggling with something in her life, let's say depression, and she wanted to keep it hidden. Following that thread, let's say she was taking some medications for it that reacted on her in an unexpected way. And then let's say that, in a public place, some people at a nearby table brought up unconscious memories in the offender sister of something long stored and hidden away. And then let's say the offender sister internally reacted to some unclaimed pieces of shadow material, albeit unconscious of doing that, and out came some comments that were *totally unrelated to the content of what was actually said!* Does that make sense?

Now let's look at the victim sister who reacted so strongly, and is still reacting even more strongly as the years go by. We have already seen how an external factor, in this case it will be the offender sister, is not responsible for what happens internally, in this case with the victim sister. It is, in fact, the victim who is not looking at what is going on internally! Why her reaction? There have to be unclaimed traits or characteristics, or locked-away memories, within the victim by virtue of the fact that she had such a strong and held-on-to reaction. What was it that was triggered in her unconscious? How much of what was said was perhaps something the victim simply did not want to hear, regardless of whether what was said was "true" in the mind of the victim? How much of the idealistic bubble within a certain realm of the victim's family ideology was shattered, resulting in her angry, vindictive reaction?

Immediately, if the opportunity arose to verbalize this, I am quite certain the victim sister would once again release, in a fury, all of the things the offender sister had said and how awful they were, ending with a comment about what a dreadful person the offender sister is and how she never wants to speak to her again. And so the story stays imbedded, with no chance of ever being released. The only way there can be resolution is for there to be an acknowledgement, by each person, of their own less than perfect humanness, including smelly socks and evil thoughts.

Turning this around for the victim would be in seeing this external event, in this case the offender, as a gift from God—an invitation, as it were, to explore and get to know more denied pieces of self. You might ask why that's of any value, and my answer would be that it will simply make you feel joyful. I have mentioned elsewhere that the beliefs—and, of course, our beliefs are being challenged when we react—are all false and they are our chains of limitation. As I see it, as have many sages and wise ones for eons, these false beliefs veil the heart. The more false beliefs are released, the more open the heart becomes and the more the love of the essence of who you are shines through. It is not that your essence has ever gone anywhere. It hasn't. It is simply that the veils covering the heart have become so layered with the beliefs that the light appears to shine less.

The ancient Egyptians spoke to "the heart weighing lighter than a feather." The chains of our beliefs are heavy, and as they are released and the veils drop away, the heart indeed becomes lighter. In Adyashanti's words, "Love is wisdom and wisdom is love." As the heart lightens the natural state of joy and well-being becomes your experience. So that's why.

I could carry this on further, but I believe I've made my point. Rather, upon reading this, if you are holding on to any story in which you will not forgive someone for something they said or did, hopefully you are now willing to look at it from a bigger perspective. As I've said a number of times, if this were your last day, would hanging on to the story still be so important? Or would the realization that you could literally carry this to your grave be enough to break the illusion that someone did something to you?

The ability to forgive or not forgive is like an argument. Can an argument ever be won? If so, who will win? Isn't an argument really that, regardless of what is being argued over, one person/country/religion is right while the other is wrong? Wars stem from this; political parties exist because of this duality; friendships and families come apart because one person wants to be right and the other wrong.

We live in a dualist Universe—we have right only because there is wrong. The very existence of the words comes from the duality. What is so outrageous about all of this is that, given an argument, I will never let you be right nor will you allow me to make you wrong. Pretty simple!

Arguments, for me, now seem futile and actually ridiculous. I see no need for them and hence I don't have them in my life. When I have a reaction—which is often what is behind the argument in the first place—then it is my call to look at myself and uncover what was stirred up in me that created the reaction. At the same time, as I become aware of my reaction, I can respond with something like "that's an interesting perspective, I have that, too." In saying that, I have acknowledged that my reaction is coming from my beliefs and that, at the other pole of this belief, I also hold the perspective of the other.

Then forgiveness happens! There is nothing to say or do; it's an inside job. The task is now to greet the person from your knowing. The tree of ignorance is opposite to the tree of knowing, the deep inner wisdom.

CHAPTER ELEVEN:

God Doesn't Care What You Wear

All religions, all this singing, one song. The differences are just illusion and vanity. The sun's light looks a little different on this wall than it does on that wall, and a lot different on this other one, but it's still one light.

Rumi

I want to start with a disclaimer that this chapter is not for everyone. Thus far, this book, though perhaps provocative to a degree, from my perspective has been gentle in its approach, resulting, I hope, in some contemplative self-reflection for you, the reader. I am aware that this current chapter, on the other hand, will be controversial for many, perhaps even offensive, and could well create a strong reaction for some. You may decide you want to skip it altogether, although I hope not. As I have already discussed, when there is reaction rather than a response, this is an internal signal telling us that something within us has been triggered; that the deeply hidden bones of some belief have been rattled.

We all know that religion is a personal and touchy subject. Everyone has their convictions, most of which are tightly held on to as being true. Still, in my work, both with others and in my examination of myself, I see how religion is the basis for so many of our beliefs. In a sense, they set a template for other beliefs to morph from. And generally speaking, there is a self-righteousness that accompanies religious beliefs, as though "God" has clearly and unequivocally spoken to each person.

A close friend, a Buddhist, was recently telling me of having spent some time with a Lama, listening to the teachings. She referred to some people attending the class as "spiritual tourists," which I thought was a smack-on way of addressing this issue. When a person is seriously interested in stripping away the illusions and finding the internal peace that is the natural right of everyone, it usually follows that the person will be willing to go, as one of Pema Chödrön's books says, to "the places that scare you." Spiritual maturity is not wanting things to be love, light, and harmony—that belongs to the child who wants everyone and everything to be "nice."

If we seriously want to delve deeper into our internal caves, an important and necessary piece requires a willingness to ask ourselves questions and then seek answers. Such is the case with this chapter. There is no intention on my part to appear harsh, and yet, at the same time, I do want to provoke you into that place of questioning. It is only in doing so that you can begin to dismantle the chains of false beliefs. Perhaps you may be having a reaction with an immediate retort, ready to fling back to the effect that "God" should not be questioned. Yet, again, I ask you to bring yourself into your own questioning and ask, "Is this my experience or am I just parroting what I have been told is so?" Has God spoken to you with clarity, telling you what is?

I am writing this book for me because this is what is in front of me at this moment. Rather than coming from a place of: "Oh, I think I'll write a book now," I am being drawn, or you could say even compelled, to write this. Please understand, however, that I am not trying to change your beliefs. I don't know you. Even if you were to attend a workshop with me, I likely wouldn't see you again. So how you live your life does not impact my life, and this is not about trying to change you. As I've mentioned several times, I have told you of my experiences and how they have led me forward in life in the hope that these writings will stir your internal pot, that piece of you which is seeking self-knowledge. My only request of you, as I request of myself, is that you be honest, open, and willing to notice your reactions for what they are—triggers to some deeply hidden piece that is being exposed. In noticing and acknowledging the reaction for what it is, the door opens a bit, even if it's only a crack, but at least it opens, so that a bit of light can shine in.

"There is a crack, a crack in everything; that's how the light gets in," sings the poet Leonard Cohen.

What I would hope for as the condition for continuing to read this chapter is that when your button is pushed by something I say, you remain open to a willingness to stop, breathe, and then critically examine the statement. I am not attempting to preach or teach anything, and I ask you not to believe a single word I have to say. You are your one and only teacher, and your job is to answer the questions according to your own truth, not according to what someone has told you is the answer.

Although many people may argue with me, if we truly examine religion, it is seen to be man-made. The process known as Enlightenment, on the other hand, is simply awakening into our true nature, awakening to that which has always been, beyond the false concepts and illusions of reality. Being in this knowing is beyond beliefs, beyond culture or race, beyond concepts, beyond judgment, beyond comparison, and beyond the need to know. Once we assign a religion, however, to that which has always been and that has no boundaries, everything changes. Within the religious context, God has now become *personal*. God has now become the judge of right and wrong, good and bad. God is now about judgment, comparison, and the need to know, which is nothing more than an attempt to control. Once religion and the *personal* God are in place, "Thy will be done" becomes a hollow lie.

When I was first married, birth control pills had just come out. The Catholic Church was quick to declare them a grave sin, which meant Catholics were told not to take them. I was using birth control pills and still going to church at the time. This was also the period during which I was having an increasing aware-ness of my internal unease with religious dogma. On three separate occasions I went to confession to three different priests and confessed three different times that I was taking the forbidden pill. I received three answers which, though dif-ferent, were each nevertheless telling me what I was to do. At that point I real-ized I needed to live my life according to what felt right for me and not accord-ing to what an institution or person told me through their own filters. That is when I left the Catholic Church.

Taking birth control pills had been declared to be a sin. What exactly is sin, anyway? Has God defined and declared what are sins? You might be quick to say, "Yes, but what about the Ten Commandments? They define sin." My response to you is, "Do they? Are you sure of that?" Further, do you know that these were the actual words of God or that the interpretations given by man are indeed correct? It would seem man is the one who determines what constitutes sin, and that, of course, would be based on the colored glasses, the layers of filters, of those who make such declarations.

I imagine there are Universal Laws and, in my experience, there is a knowing that determines them. My internal barometer dictates my sense of "morality" and hence behavior beyond the right and wrong of beliefs, as I imagine yours does also. It is said in the commandments, "Thou shalt not kill." Yet religious and economic wars kill. Does "Thou shalt not steal" mean that the father who stole a loaf of bread to feed his starving children is condemned to hell?

God the Divine does not equal religion. God the Divine is too big for any reli-gion. God the Divine did not create religion. We constantly attempt to describe that which cannot be described, and in that effort many, myself included, use the word "God" in a more generic sense. In religion, certainly, "God" is used to describe the core of the religion, whereas "Spirituality" has become an almost mainstream catchphrase, used in an attempt to describe our connection to something bigger outside of religion.

In the end, the word itself doesn't matter. The Divine, Source, Oneness, the Infinite, Higher Power, Absolute, the Tao, Self, Source-That-Cannot-Be-Named,

Spirit, and God are all words people use according to what works for them. Regardless, the desire to describe that which we know, deeply inside ourselves, remains. It seems that in the hearts of all human beings, whether from a conscious or an unconscious perspective, there is a need—a yearning—to know that which cannot be named or understood. Even the most hardcore scientist or declared atheist, when honestly questioning, acknowledges some source of all that is (or, for those more into true spirituality, of all that is not). We can break the Universe down to the smallest possible life form, yet the question of "What is the source of this smallest particle?" continues to remain unanswered. I've seen how many people call themselves atheists when, really, they are using this term because any other way of talking about that which cannot be named smacks of religion. I totally understand. In my own case, at age twenty, after the years of witnessing gross hypocrisy within the Catholic Church, I turned my back on anything even resembling religion. If you said the words "God" or "Jesus" or "prayer" in front of me, I could instantly feel myself contract.

Do not speak to me of this God. Do not speak to me of this limiting, contrived, personal God created by man. Speak to me of your experiences of your God, God the Divine, as I tell you of mine. I am not interested in your experience as being mine; I am interested only in my experience. We cannot know God through the head. Like the seeking of one's own truth, it can come only from a knowing, a knowing by heart, in the heart—your heart. Analysis and intellectual knowledge will lead only to an attempt to understand, not lead to that which is beyond description. My heart knows of what I speak: the beauty of nature beyond words, my grandchildren's love, the eyes of a homeless person in the shelter, the eyes and tears of an African mother where language prevented any words yet our hearts merged—just as your heart knows of what you speak. When we have our own experience of dropping into our true nature, into spaciousness that is beyond beliefs and personalities, the question of a bigger, indefinable picture is apparent and unavoidable.

In the realm of Grace, Divine intervention, and Divine guidance there is no judgment of right or wrong. Source did not attach descriptions of good or bad or right or wrong. The Universal Law of Source gets filtered and distorted by our beliefs. Religion immediately produces a better-than, while Source does not. In the realm of The Divine, there is simply the such-ness, the is-ness, of all that is, unfolding as it must. When we drop into the place of thinking, we feel entitled to tell the personal God we don't like how things are unfolding, and we have dropped into our need to control. Seriously, do you think The Divine needs our help? Do you think the Source of all has made mistakes in the creation of anything: what you might call "good" or "bad"? "Thy will be done" is redundant. Most religions use a similar phrase, and everyone piously parrots it. Yet, in their lives, they want to change it because the beliefs they hold so dear include wanting life their way, regardless, thus turning the phrase into, "Thy will be done, as long as it is my way."

An investigative author wrote a best-selling non-fiction book on the murder of Pope John Paul I. This author was a dinner guest of mine many years ago. He told me that when he was in Rome, nearing completion of this highly researched book, he had a long-awaited rare appointment to be allowed into the sacred library hidden in the bowels of the Vatican See. His assistant with him, this author started the car to head for this appointment only to have the car explode from a bomb. He suffered serious injuries and his assistant was killed.

All in God's Name.

When I read Dan Brown's books that focus on the Catholic Church—*Angels and Demons* and *The Da Vinci Code*—I was struck by how much of what he brought forward is true, historically and today, about both the Catholic Church and the Vatican, including the tremendous lengths the Church will go to in protecting its domain. One of the most unnerving people I have ever met was a man, who I would often by circumstance be in the company of, from the very radical arm of the Catholic Church called Opus Dei, a secret brotherhood that, it is said, will do whatever is necessary to protect the Church. I always understood Opus Dei membership to include the holiest of the Catholics, and in my beliefs at that time this would mean a warm, kind, and loving person, whereas this man was the opposite. Besides having an icy coldness to him that left me unnerved, in business he was known for his lack of ethics.

I was raised as a Catholic. I attended Catholic schools from grade school to the end of high school, with the vast majority of my teachers being nuns and the remainder lay nuns (un-ordained). I attended Mass every Sunday with my mother and went to rosary every Wednesday evening, so I know the Catholic Church. By the time I was seven, I could recite the entire Mass in Latin by heart. I loved the ritual and still do, because ritual drops me into sacred space. Nevertheless, although I loved the ritual aspects of the Church, I had great difficulty with the doctrine and the hypocrisy I was seeing through my questions.

Although I did mention some of the following earlier in the book, it seems appropriate in this context to repeat a few points. My mother was continually mortified by my behavior and the calls from teachers because of my unwillingness to capitulate. What the nuns tried with me, for eleven years of school (I skipped the last year and went to university), was to get me to simply believe what they told me I was to believe.

Recall my poignant story of when I was a six-year-old in catechism class, and I received the razor strap in front of the class for asking whether the teacher had been to Heaven? Was this nun speaking her truth when she had never had the experience of Heaven? Truth is individual and not the same for everyone, even though you've been told many times that it is. Think about it, though: what is really *your* truth? Not someone else's truth, just yours alone. And what constitutes truth, anyway? For me my truth can come only from my direct experience. What about yours? This little six-year-old was simply wanting to hear how, indeed, Heaven had been the nun's direct experience.

My experience throughout school, and yes right to the end, involved this same kind of query. I didn't get this questioning mind from my family; it seemed inherent in me. I have no idea where my questions came from; they just arose. Religion was highly illogical to me, even at such a young age. Catechism was the first class of every day and its purpose was to make you a Pope-abiding Catholic who believed what you were told, regardless of how you felt. We didn't read the Bible but rather were told what was in the Bible. Let's start with: God made everyone. Wonderful, I'll buy that. God loves everyone. Great. Well then, if God made everyone, and loves everyone, how come my neighbor isn't good enough?

Why would God create all these people and have the majority of them go to hell because they weren't Catholic? Why do I have to kill my neighbor because he sees things from a different perspective than me?

We are like blind sheep, nodding our heads in agreement, while someone of authority tells us that this is the way it is. We need to seek truth. Do you know, as in *absolutely know,* that what you say in God's Name is absolutely your truth? Yet this is the stuff of war. This is the stuff that allows people to kill one another. Are the Protestant Irish better or worse than the Catholic Irish for their points of view? Do you honestly believe God created human beings so that some are less worthy than others? Have you ever sincerely thought about this?

Some of the most unkind, inhumane acts of humanity throughout history have been committed in God's Name. Let's just take a look at the Spanish Inquisition of the Catholic Church. The Inquisition was a massive cleansing of the Church to rid it of any and all infidels who dared to believe anything other than what the Holy See was telling them to believe. The most horrific, unspeakable cruelties were done, all in God's Name. People were thrown into boiling pots of oil, people were sliced from throat to groin and their organs pulled out of their breathing bodies, people were tied to the stake and burned alive, people had their bodies literally torn apart—limb by limb—on a wheel. While all of this was being done to humans, by humans, families including children were forced to watch. It is happening in our world now, just the institution is different. Yet it is all in God's Name: "Believe what I tell you to or I will kill you."

The title of this book is *God Doesn't Care What You Wear.* For me this short phrase says everything about the core of this book, and provokes deep self-examination. Although I had had religious women in my classes before, let me tell you about my first experience of having veiled, covered religious women. One of these wore four layers of clothing because she felt she was so unworthy and so unclean. Following a session I had done in class on one of these women, there were several questions. Then one of the veiled women started to talk about the whys of the veils, robes, and covering of the body and head in general. I listened with respect as she described their beliefs around required clothing for women and then, out of my mouth came: "Do you really think God cares what you wear?" Wow! That was one profound statement when I heard it, and from the looks on the faces of the students I imagine it was also for them. Does God care what you wear? Do you absolutely know for certain, as your truth, that what you wear matters to God?

Of course I'm using clothing as an example, but it's not just about clothing. Not at all. It is about anything that makes us self-righteous or holier-than-thou. Is your way to The Divine more accurate than mine? Does depriving yourself of the fruits of life make you better than? Can your God only be honored by religion practiced in an institution? Does God care what you eat? Does being vegetarian assure you greater spiritual rewards than those who eat animals? (If being vegetarian feels right for you, that's another story.)

It's *about all of the beliefs that surround religion* and what separates religions, what separates people, one from the other. The question isn't whether or not you consider yourself religious. If belonging to an organized religion works for you, great. Being in community, as one is in belonging to a church, is a driving human need. Nevertheless, honestly ask, "Are God the Divine and religion synonymous?" Where does religion come from? Who started religion, anyway? I realize many people reading this will have answered for themselves already, yet it serves as a reminder of how quickly we buy into someone else's beliefs. I ask only that you be open enough to ask yourself some questions and allow the answers to come forward. Examine this: what religion on planet Earth do you know for certain was made by God? Perhaps it's of value to point out that Jesus was not a Christian, Abraham was not a Jew, Mohammed was not a Muslim, and Buddha was not a Buddhist. Is it not obvious that the wide variety of religions, numbering literally in the hundreds, have come about because a human being has declared one religion as being not quite right, according to *their* beliefs, so they form their own, thus getting what they want?

According to the World Christian Encyclopedia, "There are 19 major religions, which are subdivided into a total of 270 large religious groups and many smaller ones." So how are religions formed, and why? Answer that for yourself. What makes a religion necessary? Why do you want to belong to a religion? If your answer is because you feel safe and want to feel part of a community, then you might examine that. It's not about anything being right or wrong, and examining does not mean you leave that which nourishes you. In searching for what is true for you, if you investigate, you'll see that all religions have been created by humanity with a personal God, not God the Divine, and moreover, all have fear as their fundamental base, thus the rules. "If you do this everything will be okay," and "if you don't live this way then you're in big trouble." And we actually allow ourselves to be led, by a ring in our nose, into the corral of like behavior. Catholics and Jews and Muslims and Buddhists and all the other institutions have pursued these fear concepts. Different names for different folks: there is "Purgatory," where everyone but the saints will have to spend some time suffering. And there is "Hell," the place of no return. Does it really feel true to you that God would impose these concepts? How special does it make you feel that you're good enough to get to "Heaven" whereas *you know for sure* your neighbor is not?

Jesus, in *The Gospel of Thomas* said: "If you bring forth what is within you, what you bring forth will save you. If you do not bring forth what is within you, what you do not bring forth will destroy you."

Many wise individuals have lived on Earth and left their imprint. The wisdom came from their own process of self-examination and not from someone else. Elaine Pagels is an acclaimed Gnostic gospels scholar and professor of religious studies. She has participated with other scholars in editing several sacred texts from Nag Hammadi, written at the time of Jesus, that did not come through the censorship of the Church. Professor Pagels writes, based on these teachings of Jesus, "So this gnosis is self-knowledge … it's a question of knowing who you really are … knowing yourself at a deep level. The secret of gnosis is that when you know yourself at that level you will also come to know God, because you will discover that the Divine is within you." Then, in The Gospel of Thomas, Jesus said: "The Kingdom of God is within you and outside of you." In Luke 6:31, it is written, "Do unto others as you would have them do unto you." These few statements are utterly profound. Know thyself. This means honest self-examination to see and honor all that makes you human. And just imagine the world if everyone lived according to what they would want done unto them.

Be true to yourself, not to someone else! Polonius in Shakespeare's *Hamlet* says it perfectly and succinctly with: "To thine own self be true."

Some Christians are adamant that Christianity was born at the death of Jesus, yet the reality is that it took a few hundred years before people formed the religion of Christianity. Jesus didn't ask for it, Jesus didn't form it, God the Divine didn't form it. Human beings formed Christianity. Yes, there were followers of this wise man, men who preached his words, but it was only when it became advantageous to control the masses through doctrine that Christianity was born. The original words, as passed on through various renditions of various bibles, have been selected and altered according to the filters and beliefs of those writing their versions and their particular interpretation. The same is true for the teachings of Judaism, Islam, and Buddhism.

This has to come back to living your own truth. If it's your truth, wouldn't that mean you would live it all the time? During my childhood I knew a Catholic family with many children and lots of money. The children and mother went to church every single day, and the father went for sure on Sundays and sometimes during the week. They had a live-in couple working for them who were illegals. This wealthy couple paid these people, who served them, a small amount compared with what they would have to pay a legal couple. They went to church all the time, and had a large family according to what the church said they needed to do. Just don't ask them to pay someone more than they need to!

Many years ago I was on a flight from a religious city in the Middle East, sitting in the first-class section. I was the only non-Arab woman on the plane, and I was not veiled. This section was full and, as I recall, nearly every man, if not all, had a woman sitting with him. As we were leaving from this holy city, all the women were completely covered with burkas, veils on their faces, and a few wearing leather masks. I was treated very rudely and served with reluctance only after all the others had been served, even though I had been in their country as a guest of the King. The women were required to eat under their veils lest any man on the plane get a glimpse of their skin. As we were landing in Geneva, I was watching the women and could see them fidgeting with their bags and looking at themselves in a mirror under the veils. Then, literally as the back wheels of the plane made their first contact with the Geneva runway, the masks, veils, and burkas flew off! By the time the front wheels hit the tarmac, all that could be seen were very glamorous women wearing haute couture dresses, spike heels, bright lipstick, and insanely expensive jewelry. Later, in five-star Geneva restaurants, I can assure you they did not have to eat under a veil. If "God" had told them they had to cover themselves, did that only apply on planes and in their own country?

During this trip, I went to the old souk (market) with the wife of one of the key Ministers of the country. Given that I was in a religious country plus going to the old souk, it was mandatory that I put on a burka. This one even had the hands sewn shut so that they could not be revealed, and I had a veil over my face. In those days I still wore high heels. Between my shoes and the veil I found it increasingly difficult to walk on the old cobbled streets of the souk, at which point my companion suggested I hold the veil in such a way that only my eyes could be seen: no hair, no skin, just my blue eyes showing. Three separate times, I had a man step in front of me, blocking my way as he angrily shook his fist within inches of hitting my face while shouting, "Woman, cover your face!" It was only because my companion responded with, "She is a guest of our King and not of Allah" that he stepped aside to let me pass.

Does God care what I wear?

A couple of years back, there were two South African women visiting Nigeria. There they heard about a pregnant woman who was going to be buried up to her head, then stoned until her head was smashed open. She was to receive this punishment of death because ten men had raped her and she had become pregnant. The men who had raped her were those who would be smashing her head with rocks because it was her fault she had become pregnant out of marriage. These South African women, on hearing of this, sent out emails to their women friends, who then started a mass-mailing campaign around the world. The pressure became such that the government stepped in and the woman was saved.

Young girls have their genitals brutally mutilated with broken bottles or razor blades so they can never know sexual pleasure while being raped by men who own them.

All in God's Name.

As Mahatma Gandhi said: "Before the throne of the Almighty, man will be judged not by his acts but by his intentions. For God alone reads our hearts."

To many, the United States is a Christian country. Is it? I imagine the many millions of non-Christians born in the USA would disagree. Yet there was a raving minister of some Christian church on TV recently screaming that if you believed in Buddha, or Mohammed, or anyone other than Jesus Christ, you should "get out!" I experienced a similar situation when I challenged a couple of students in Northern Ireland—who just happened to be radical IRA members—over the division of their island. I felt an old fear not of this lifetime come up in me on seeing the pure hatred, the stone-throwing type, wanting to annihilate me.

For the Love of God, because "God" said that Catholics are going to Heaven and Protestants to Hell, or the other way around if you are Protestant. Or a Jew. Or even better yet, an Orthodox Jew. Or a Muslim.

I know all life is created equal. No one needs to tell me that; it is a life-long knowing for me. Logic itself says that, given that some Divine Source created all that is. Knowing that life unfolds without my assistance, however, is not an excuse to allow me to sit back and keep my mouth shut about atrocities to women, whether they be Muslims, Indians, or indigenous. Indeed, knowing the sacredness of all life makes it ever more important in my eyes to help bring awareness to these injustices, for anything less than equality is an injustice. There is no place in me where I will tolerate women being killed for the senseless satisfaction of men.

As Bishop Tutu said, "If you are neutral in situations of injustice, you have chosen the side of the oppressor." In the case of injustice, I choose to be on the side seeking equality versus that of the oppressor. My grandmother, and probably yours also, would say, "There but for the Grace of God go I." Although my hand dealt did not include my living in an oppressive climate, that does not give me the right to ignore those who are oppressed.

I would be untrue to myself if I did not acknowledge here that I recognize that many of these women are simply not allowed to live their truth and are unable to stand up for themselves. I know of many ugly stories of what happens if women do try to rebel or break away from these communities and others around the world. All I can do is support them as a sister, and by telling a bit of their story.

According to John 8:32, "The truth will set you free."

AMEN!

CHAPTER TWELVE:

Don't Cry For Me, Argentina

Your time is limited, so don't waste it living someone else's life. Don't be trapped by dogma, which is living with the results of other people's thinking. Don't let the noise of others' opinions drown out your own inner voice. And, most important, have the courage to follow your heart and intuition... They somehow already know what you truly want to become. Everything else is secondary.

Steve Jobs, from his Stanford University address

Although no single experience is more powerful than the next, the following story is a remarkable example of the magic of my life-script unfolding in spite of me.

As I mentioned in my chapter that included The Dark Shaman, my close friend and I had organized a trip to the northern part of the Amazon. One of the women from that trip called me a few months later saying she was planning to see Mother Meera in Germany, and would I go with her? Our group included myself and three other women from various parts of North America. After meeting in Frankfurt, we rented a car to drive to the small town where Mother Meera lives and sits Darshan according to a schedule.

Darshan is when one sits in the presence of one who is said to be a revered holy person, and in doing so, receives a blessing. Sitting Darshan with Mother Meera is a silent ritual during which those present go forward one at a time, when it feels appropriate, and kneel in front of her. Mother Meera then touches the person's head and looks into their eyes, thus imparting a blessing. At the very least, this experience is a wonderful gift, and more usually, it is a very powerful experience for the participant.

We sat Darshan for the three days it was being offered at this time. The third day happened to be Easter Sunday and, as we were reasonably close to the city of Cologne with its famously beautiful cathedral, and given that we were finished with Darshan in the early morning, we decided to go to Mass in the cathedral, followed by an outrageously elegant lunch. I was quite resistant about going to Mass. Much as I loved the ritual of the Catholic Church, since leaving it many years before I had not been near a church and really had no desire to be either. However, it was the group choice, and so I went.

This stunningly gorgeous setting for Mass, accompanied by a choir of angel voices, melted even my cynicism, while the history of the cathedral itself added to the making of a very powerful experience.

During World War II, the British were using every tactic possible to defeat the Germans. Cologne, sitting on both sides of the Rhine, was a city that prided itself on its beauty, and the cathedral, built in 1248, was a particularly treasured jewel. The British attitude was that if they could defeat the will of the German people, it would help defeat the country as a whole, and to that end, they mercilessly bombed Cologne. The photographs of the destruction of the city are heartbreaking, while the picture of the cathedral left standing is exalting! Literally all the buildings surrounding the cathedral were destroyed, yet the bombs barely touched the church. Could it be that the unknown protectors were the angels, hidden in the niches, circling the upper rim of the cathedral?

Destiny entered when, heading back to our car following lunch, we turned the corner of the cathedral square and found ourselves in front of a group of street musicians from the Andes, the mountains of South America. My eyes locked in instantaneous connection with a man selling the CDs of the group as we spontaneously started to dance. Long curly black hair, tied back, framed his brown face while his warm dancing eyes, engaging smile, and sensual energy wrapped me in. Our dance lasted only a few minutes in physical time, yet much longer it seemed in universal time. While we conversed in Spanish for the entire dance, our conversation contained only short bits of actual information—"I'm from Canada." "I'm from Argentina." Along with his first name—nothing more than these few tidbits. When we stopped dancing, he asked if I would go for coffee with him. I explained I couldn't as I was with friends and we were leaving for Frankfurt. He asked "Then when?" to which he added, "We need to talk." I could only reply, "I'm sorry, we're driving to Frankfurt now and I'm leaving for Canada in the morning," and I walked away.

When we got into the car, being aware of this special connection I had had with this man, I commented on how I felt he had something for me. We all agreed on the incredible obvious energy between the two of us. Had I made a mistake in leaving? Throughout our drive to Frankfurt, we women talked and talked about this until I finally declared the story was finished.

The Universe, however, had a different scene in my script. Once I got back to Canada I started having dreams that included this man from Argentina. Although I'm not someone who explores the meaning of my dreams in detail every day, I do pay attention. He was in my dreams several times a week. As the dreams began to intensify, they often seemed to include a strong shamanic content. As with my Dark-Shaman friend, I finally gave in, recognizing how the dreams were speaking to me.

After a month of these dreams, I awoke one morning with an inner message—I would return to Germany to see if I could find this man. "Are you friggin' crazy?" my logical piece internally screamed at me. "Okay," I replied, in my bargaining logical voice to the inner voice, "*If* I am to go to Germany to find this person I need some signs." With a challenging and skeptical attitude, I started to look for flights. I had some strict criteria around all this, because my first grandchild was expected in a few weeks, which meant that not only would I need to leave almost immediately, I could also allow myself to be gone for only one week. Regular airfares at such short notice were way too high, when suddenly I found a charter fare (and I *never* fly charter) on the exact same flight for which the regular fares were prohibitive, leaving the next day in the evening! It also *just so happened* this was the last charter seat available, and at an unbelievably low fare, so I grabbed it. The charter conditions meant I would have to return in a week, so it was all perfect. Not a few days before and not a few days after, just one week.

I then realized I had to tell my two sons what I was doing. "Well, it's like this. I'm going to Frankfurt, then I'm going to drive to Cologne, then I'm going to wander the streets looking for this street musician person who I don't know, whose last name I don't know, who lives I don't know where." In my story creation, I was imagining my sons declaring me certifiable and going to court to say I was no longer able to handle my life affairs.

Deep breath and into the car. As I started the ignition, the radio came on, which is always on CBC, a classical radio station. The announcer, discussing the next piece, finished his commentary with "and this piece of *musica antiqua* [early music] is coming to you from Cologne Cathedral." "Okay, okay, okay," I laughed. "I get the message." When I arrived at my son's house, where he and my other son were working on preparing the house for my soon-to-arrive granddaughter, I announced my departure the next day along with my short story. My eldest, the soon-to-be father, said something like "Are you 'effing crazy?!" adding, "Well, it's your life, so if this is what you have to do, this is what you have to do," while my younger son said: "Hey, go for it—I hope it's great!"

Whew! I got away without being institutionalized. That went a lot better than all the thoughts I had had about how it could have gone. Nevertheless, the next day, flying all night to Frankfurt, I was a wreck. Forget what anyone else thought, my internal critic was sufficiently relentless with non-stop chatter, chastising and judging me, so that I was increasingly becoming convinced I truly was nuts (whatever that is in the conventional world.)

Landing in Frankfurt, I rented a car. Now realize, please, this was before the days of GPS (or at least of my knowing about it), combined with the fact that, GPS or not, I hadn't even thought to look at a map. I prefer that someone else read the map for me and, besides, I hadn't had time to purchase one. (As an aside, I *am* known by my friends to be a good bird-dogger, which means I tend to "smell" things out or, said another way, I just seem to know which way to go.)

So, when I drove off out of Frankfurt airport, knowing only that I was heading to Cologne, with my self-critic (and there is no better!) plus no map, it was with more than a degree of trepidation. On top of it all, I knew nothing of the city layout of Cologne, much less where to stay. Nevertheless, thanks to the gods and angels, when I arrived in Cologne I knew I wanted to stay in the center, so all I did was follow the signs. Voilà, there I was in the old section, looking up at a quaint little hotel. This would be my home for my days in Cologne.

Settled in, I just tried to relax into what it was that I was there for. I actually slept soundly that night, even though I recall it was probably from utter emotional and physical exhaustion from the trans-Atlantic trip and drive, rather than from any sense of saneness or internal peace.

The next morning I woke up with "This is crazy, crazy, beyond crazy!" shouting at me. Seriously, what was I doing here? Yet, undeniably (at least from my point of view), it seemed I was supposed to be here.

"NOW WHAT?" came my insane scream.

About halfway through the month of my increasing dreams, one of the women from our Mother Meera group had mailed me a couple of photographs of myself and Señor Argentina dancing. What a surprise! Although I hadn't been aware of anyone taking photos, these would prove to be very useful in Cologne. At the time of receiving them, though, it was reassuringly validating to see, even in the photos, the energy and connection of the two of us.

I have awareness around illegal immigrants and their underground networking, perhaps, in part, from having lived in South America and perhaps also just because I do. This awareness was needed when I went looking for this elusive man.

Clutching my photos, I wandered the streets of Cologne. When I would see a Latino, I would politely stop them, explain what I was doing while showing the photo: "I am here from Canada and I just need to talk to him. All I want is twenty minutes, nothing more. Here is the card for the hotel where I am staying and my room number—please ask him to call me."

This was my daily routine, wandering the streets, stopping and asking every man or woman from Latin America. In the evenings, I gave up any idea of the search and I would always find a pleasant restaurant. I was deciding between three restaurants for dinner one evening, yet when I left my hotel I still didn't know which one I would go to. My body just followed where my feet took me and there I was. The maître d', having asked if I was alone, sat me at a table with my back against the wall. While sipping wine and reading, I noticed a man being seated at the table for two next to me. Though we hadn't acknowledged each other, I was soon aware he had a nice presence. He was reading a Herald Tribune, which, in my old days, I read religiously. When he put it back in the pocket of his tweed jacket, I asked if he minded if I read it, explaining I hadn't read an English paper in several days. "Not at all. Please," as he passed it to me. As I was interested in only a couple of sections, I soon handed the paper back to him, which was when we had our first eye connection. This warm engaging man and I ended up enjoying our dinners together, sipping red wine, and chatting for hours as we relaxed into comfortable sharing. He heard and was intrigued by my story of looking for Señor Argentina as our conversation continued way past dessert and cognac. Eventually we went walking arm-in-arm in the night streets of Cologne, heading toward the cathedral, enjoying our new-found friendship. My companion, an architect, is well versed in European architecture, so it was a bit of a surprise when I said, "Don't you just love the protective angels around the top?" and he replied with, "No, there are no angels on the outside perimeter." "Oh yes there are! Come on, I'll show you!" So there we were, staring up at the angels hidden in the niches, indeed circling the outer perimeter of the cathedral.

Besides our obvious comfort with each other, we were also noting and enjoying our mutual attraction. Given other circumstances, who knows what would have happened. But at that time, I was on a mission and not open to any diversion. Still, when we parted in the very early morning, we agreed that if I did not find Señor Argentina, we would consider hooking up for a few days.

As I was beginning to write this section, the memories of that evening came flooding back. Nineteen years later, with the wonder of the Internet, I was able to find him and send an email message. What seemed almost instant, I received a lovely reply calling my note "a gift from heaven." We reignited our flame for a bit before snuffing it out again. During our conversations, though, we discussed the angels around the upper perimeter of the cathedral. After considerable research, my friend said he could find no architectural evidence of angels in the upper niches of the Cologne Cathedral even though we had stood looking up at them that one beautiful and memorable evening.

Back to the mission at hand. Not a single person on the streets gave even a flicker of the eye to let me know they knew Señor Argentina, yet I knew they did. And I knew he would call me. Early in the morning of the fourth day, following my evening with the architect, the phone in my room rang, just as I was to get into the shower. "Who are you? Why are you trying to find me?" he growled. "I only want to speak with you for like twenty minutes," I said. "I don't want anything. We danced a month ago. I'm from Canada." Instantly the world changed. "I'll be at your hotel by 2 o'clock," he said.

And there began the next phase of my life. He is a kind lovely human being with a big heart. He's smart, he's a survivor, and he was a challenge! As our time together unfolded, I heard various pieces of his story, many of which touched me deeply. His parents were Chilean, part Mapuche (the most numerous group of Chilean indigenous peoples.) His father worked in the Anaconda mines and was responsible for instigating a group protesting the conditions of the mines. A price was placed on his life, forcing him, along with his friends, to leave Chile. His mother was pregnant with my friend when his father left to make the treacherous crossing into Argentina. Neither he nor his friends—there were either seven or eight, I don't recall exactly—had winter clothes, jackets, or boots as they literally walked over the Andean mountains on their grueling journey. Most froze, dying from exposure, and only two survived—my friend's father and his best friend. Eventually the mother was able to come by bus to Argentina with her six other children and gave birth to my friend in Argentina.

The father died shortly before my friend's birth, leaving the mother destitute and struggling to provide for her family. She woke every morning at 4:00, set bread to rise for one of her daughters to bake later, walked for one and a half hours before she could get a bus, all to be at work in someone's home by early morning. She worked for a wealthy family who threw food in the garbage every meal, yet never was she offered any to take to her starving family. And we dare to wonder how revolutionaries and "terrorists" are born!

During the revolution in Argentina, my friend's brother was shot in the town square and my friend had a price on his head. He managed to get out of Argentina, to Europe, arriving penniless, scared, and depressed. He would not return to Argentina for many years. As the records of the dissidents were still active, any attempt to enter the country would have meant his immediate arrest. His mother died without once again seeing her favorite son, while he raged inside at the injustice.

In the time just before I met him, or shortly after, a group of dissidents managed to get into the government building where all the damning paperwork was kept on those who had participated against the regime. All the documents were burned! This was freedom for people like my friend, who could now apply for passports and finally return home. My friend's first visit back to Argentina was with me—as you can imagine, a very emotional return.

For those of us who don't know this level of poverty, the cemetery where my friend's father is buried was a great leveler for me. In Latin American countries, the cemetery is visibly divided into those who could afford a proper burial and those who could not, with a wide range in the bell of the curve. My friend's father was at the absolute bottom of the curve. His body, wrapped only in a sheet, had been placed in the dirt with a simple wooden cross marking the spot and a circle of stones in the shape of the grave. Our visit to his grave was a very moving experience for me, and one I am reliving as I write. After finding the spot, we went to the paint store for some minimal supplies, and when we returned, my friend slowly and lovingly painted each of the rocks with white paint. Having repaired the little wooden cross, he sat and talked to his father, as did I. Just as we were about to walk away, on this hot quiet windless day, a tremendous gust of wind blew through. Looking at each other, no words were necessary, though later he said he had felt great comfort from the wind.

Someone asked me recently if I returned to look for Señor Argentina because of some burning flame of desire, for which the answer is an absolute no. Truly, when I went back, it was because I felt compelled to talk to him, to find out something from him, even though I had not a clue what that might be. When we finally did meet that afternoon for coffee, there were no questions left. Instead, there was a mutual knowing of a deep connection between us that cannot be explained, and for which it would be foolhardy to try.

This relationship was so completely contrary to any I had had in the past and, as with the Dark Shaman, certainly not one I could have ever imagined. Indeed, it was at the opposite pole from my last marriage. Logically, it made no sense whatsoever. We had language barriers, we had education barriers, we had economic barriers, and we had geographic barriers; yet, somehow, we managed to have a fulfilling relationship for a couple of years. In the process, I was pushed into places of my self-growth that I can't imagine having reached without my Señor Argentina as a catalyst. I looked my own prejudice in the eye. I was able to experience a level of life through his eyes that few of my friends would ever know. And although my Spanish is considered quite good, dealing with relationship issues in that language took on a whole new face.

Was it a traumatic relationship? Yes. Did it push me to my edges? You better believe it, in more ways than one can imagine. Do I have any regrets? None. From my perspective, every challenge, every button pushed, is a gift from God. My only participation is whether or not I'm open to seeing the gift.

Although it's not always my response to my experiences, I do try to stay out of the place of needing to know. What I mean by that is that I don't try to figure out why something happened or how someone came into my life. My preference, although admittedly not always successfully accomplished, is to let me follow my life rather than try to lead my life from some place that appears logical. Later, once I was able to look back on this relationship, this phase of my life, I was able to see this as a gift of incredible proportions. The awe of this life chapter has never left me. Could I have orchestrated such a scene of my movie on my own? Hardly! The story unfolded in spite of me. Yes, there was my participation, coming from saying "yes," and yes some of the decisions along the way caused a few major detours, yet the unfolding continued.

And eventually it was time. What I needed to get out of the relationship was complete, and I was not willing to continue in what had become for me a compromise to my truth.

CHAPTER THIRTEEN:

"What If's" and Regrets Turned Into "I'm So Grateful For's"

When you change the way you look at things, the things you look at change.

Wayne Dyer

Long ago I determined that I did not want to die with regrets in my life basket. For me this has included following through when I have an internal message about something. It doesn't mean I always get a clear message, because often my own filters muddy the airwaves; yet it does mean I pay attention. We all have intuition. The question is, what do we do when we get an intuitive hit? If we notice the intuition and then use our mind to reason why we "shouldn't do that," the moment is lost. Intuition requires a trusting that includes a follow-through with action, otherwise we may be headed for a rocky detour.

Along with paying attention, there appears to be, as I've mentioned in other chapters, an unfolding that brings us from one experience to our next significant life experience. We notice what is in front of us and act or, as is often the case, we take a detour (a.k.a. discover the consequences) in relation to a particular issue. Actually, we frequently take multiple detours around the same issue, each one a bit more uncomfortable and tortuous than the last, because we refuse to acknowledge what awareness life is asking of us. The detour ends only when we come to the understanding that we are repeating a pattern. Nevertheless, regardless of how many detours I have had, I have come to know that I receive what is perfectly next for me. Life doesn't care whether I like it or not, or whether I kick and scream and cry in protest about how it shouldn't be. I can go with what is being shown to me or I can decide to ignore the message and suffer the consequences of detours. If I choose to suffer—and remember, no one causes the suffering other than me to me—that, too, appears to be part of my unfolding. Out of this, I have learned to trust life, so that it is not about "Why did this happen as it did?" but rather, as I am quickly brought into the pattern, being willing to examine myself and see what life is asking of me and, from that, to see the magnificence of the unfolding.

It was a great realization when I could feel into, with a heart-knowing, the greatness of all life's unfoldings, to see that nothing occurs uselessly. Nothing occurs uselessly! Everything changed for me from that moment on. So although I do have a few regrets, thankfully they are not a big item in my life.

My last marriage, where I played in the field of the jet-setters and the big boys, was an enormous gift in myriad ways. I have had a dear friend for nearly forty years with whom I have shared most of my growth experiences. Had I not been in that marriage, I don't imagine I would have met her, given that our lives, until we met, were vastly different, socially and economically, not to mention that we lived a great geographical distance from each other. The circumstances were such that it was only because of, and through, our husbands that we were introduced. She has been a significant person in my life, as I believe I have been in hers, and it has been humbling to see the perfection of this particular piece of my life mosaic. We have been mutual support for each other as we dared to dip our toes in new waters, exploring and expanding our points of view on life, contrary to our families. It seems we've almost taken turns encouraging each other to learn a new modality or to see a particular perspective. This dear friend has been a wonderful life gift.

Relationships often seem to be an area where we experience what-ifs. There's the "if only I hadn't said..." or the "if he/she had just been..." or "it wouldn't have happened if he/she hadn't been at that party." Idealization is often behind regrets—for example, in marriage, where the belief is that it will last forever. Such was the case with my first marriage. I want to be sensitive in saying this next piece, yet I don't know if that's possible because each of you will have your own interpretation. Nevertheless, this was an important scene in my movie.

I married young. He and I were good friends at university, and, at that time had some things in common. When we were going to get married, a male friend of mine whom I had dated a bit said to me, "Don't get married, it won't last. Come to Europe with me and travel for a year." My reply was, "I know you're right. I do know I'll get divorced. But I know I am meant to have children, and if I don't do it now, I can see that I won't do it later."

The two children I have from this marriage have been major stabilizers in my life. They also represent one important area where I feel some regret. Oddly, the regret isn't that I did anything "wrong" as a parent, rather that in being so shut down myself, I was not really available to them emotionally, to be aware of their challenges and to offer guidance from insightful awareness.

I have only recently started communicating a bit with a man who has been dear to my heart since I was a teenager, which makes it a very long time ago that we first met. As I was reviewing a particular aspect of my life, I was remembering him from a place I hadn't quite reached fully before. More of that in a minute, after I give you some necessary background.

My father became a partner with several others in a land deal. One business associate, who lived about 500 miles from me, had a daughter a year older than myself and we became good friends. The state where this family lived had a driving age of only fifteen, whereas for me it was sixteen, and a year to a teen can be a very big thing. I had learned to drive a car when I was twelve—my dad being my driving instructor—so that by the time I reached fifteen, I was actually a very good driver and quite capable. As I say that, it's more than a bit shocking for me to remember the twelve-year-old driving around the neighborhood (and no further!), but things truly were quite different in those days.

Right after my fifteenth birthday, which just happened to coincide with my going to visit my friend, I took my driver's test, taking advantage of the lower age there and because I could use her address. I was super-excited to get my license at fifteen because it meant I almost had my own car. Little kids have big memories, and every year I reminded my dad of a promise he had made on my sixth birthday, "You can pick out a car on your sixteenth birthday." I never forgot that! So it was then, less than a year after receiving my driver's license, that this somewhat precocious, strong-minded girl went car shopping on her own. Remember, it was very different back then. This just-about-to-turn sixteen-year-old went to the car dealership that sold Austin-Healeys, convinced the dealers I was a sincere shopper with a valid driver's license, and test-drove a fabulously beautiful turquoise convertible, top down of course, to our house, where my dad was pleasantly enjoying his lunch. Bursting into the house with uncontainable excitement I shouted, "Come on, come on, come daddy; I'll take you for a ride. You are going to love this car!" While my flabbergasted, furious mother was shouting at my dad about how I would kill myself with a car like that, and demanding that my dad was absolutely not to give in to my coercion, we roared away. The car had a stick shift—where had I learned to drive that?—which meant it had a particularly kicky, fun acceleration. My dad, gripping his almost-always-worn fedora hat, his sports coat flapping in the open convertible, all the while chomping down on his practically-never-without-it cigar in his mouth, couldn't resist laughing and enjoying the ride. Me, too! It was one of the best rides ever. Well, the fun was short-lived. Even though I knew I had convinced my dad that this was to be the car he promised long ago, that ended as we pulled into the driveway. We were met by my now thoroughly enraged mother, who threatened my dad with: "If you dare even consider buying this car for her..." It was obvious my dad understood the rest of the sentence. No Austin-Healey for me, although I did get a convertible, albeit it a much less kicky automatic-transmission car, after sufficiently hounding my dad with, "But you promised, you promised." Not getting that sports car probably saved my life, although it has taken almost until now in my life to come to that realization.

The next scene in this part of my movie involves my driving down, in my new car, shortly after my birthday, to see my friend 500 miles away. Her mother—a serious alcoholic—could and would turn from her naturally acerbic nature into a truly vicious person within one or two drinks. A few years earlier, she had lost her youngest daughter to cancer, and perhaps the bitterness of what she deemed an unfair dealing of the hand of God came out most when she was drinking.

My friend was madly in love at age 17 and planning on marrying the fellow, so she said. I remember just being teenage-happy for her, simply because she seemed so happy. Meanwhile her mother was furious, doing whatever she could to break this relationship off and, in turn, furious with me for being supportive. In the end, I got caught in the crossfire.

Although some of the details are fuzzy, I remember that my friend invited a bunch of other friends over to her house for a pool party one night. After that, we all went out dancing, and we got home late but still within the curfew set by her mother. None of that mattered because her mother was very drunk and insanely furious. My friend and I both did our naïve teenage best to placate her and quickly made our way to bed.

I don't know how many hours I had been asleep. I only remember that I was in a deep sleep when I woke to my friend's mother screaming at me, swaying in her drunken state, waving a gun at me. She was telling me how I was no good, nothing but a rotten whore (a horrifying word, even though I wasn't even sure what it meant), adding that I didn't deserve to live. "Why do you get to live when you don't deserve it and my little girl is dead?" Even though the charge is gone from this as I write, I am nevertheless still able to feel how devastating it was for me at the time. The self-deprecation I felt from believing what she said about me, coupled with feeling all my life that I didn't fit in, became a formula for suicide.

I don't remember exactly, but I think my friend's dad came into the room, wrenched the gun from his wife, and got her out of the room. Very early in the morning I grabbed my things, got into my car, and started to drive: an emotion-ally torn-up sixteen-year-old, feeling worthless, told she was a very bad person, on the road, driving alone with 500 miles to go. This is the only time I can recall when I played with the idea of suicide. I drove much faster than I normally would on the narrow two-lane highway, because the US state I was in didn't (and still doesn't) have a speed limit. I remember I took risks and I remember that I knew I was taking risks. I was riding on the edge, toying with, unconsciously playing with, the idea of ending my life because I obviously didn't fit in.

There were no cell phones or tracking GPS's in those days, so there was no way for anyone to contact or find me. When I arrived back home, after many hours on the road, my mother was hysterically relieved to see me. My friend's mother, while barely intelligible, had called my mother in the early morning hours to tell her what a failure she had been as a mother and what a bad, evil person I was.

It was the last time my mother spoke to this woman. Shortly after, the business partnership ended. Although my dad was innately clever, he was a shake-hands businessman and not very sophisticated. It was only many years after the end of this partnership I found out about the inequitable split that left my dad receiving considerably less than his contractual portion.

It was only through writing about this that I became aware of, and able to, give my thanks to my mother for having refused to allow my dad to buy me that sports car that I had so desperately wanted. I imagine having had such a high-powered car could well have been my tipping point.

My friend did indeed decide she was going to marry, and was subsequently kicked out of her house by her deranged mother. I know my friend had some very challenging times with her mother, yet, as I was reflecting on this, I clearly see how her family life while growing up contributed greatly to who she is. I would describe her as an open hearted and compassionate person who treats almost everyone with kindness while, at the same time, she is solid in who she is and holds her ground whenever necessary. So while the perception of her childhood might be that of difficulty, it would appear the gift has been in turning her emotional difficulties into the compassionate person she is.

I continued to drive down to spend time with her and others in that town, including the person I mentioned earlier in this chapter—the man who has always held a special spot in my heart. I think he must have been born with a mission to make people laugh, because he was always doing that. What it was like for him inside, I always had a feeling, might not have always been what he presented to others. Inner suffering can often create a kind, compassionate persona.

As I was deep in writing, although not on this as-yet-uncreated chapter, I was remembering him in a sweet, yearning way. I came to a profound new realization of his gift to me. I imagine he has no idea and, then again, perhaps he does, given his behavior. I was an alive, vibrant teenager of the mature (well to me I was mature) ages of 16 to 17 when I was madly in love with this young man. He was six years older than myself, a huge gap at that time. He was unexpectedly drafted out of university and sent to a war zone. Being a typical in-love teenager, I pined away and could hardly wait until he got back. I would have had sex with him without question, and herein lies the gift. Although he seemed to be of the same sentiment as myself, he nevertheless firmly and clearly said "no." He commented on how devastating it would be if pregnancy (yes, this was before the pill) were the result, and he wasn't open to taking any chances. I imagine my being underage also played a big factor from his perspective.

The gift came in the realization of what a kind and thoughtful thing he had done. I was a naïve kid who would never have made him "wrong," looking for love in all the wrong places. Had he not put a stop to advancing intimacy, and had we continued, my life most likely would have been very different from what it has been. I remember he also wisely said something about how he wouldn't be enough for what I wanted. This good and kindly man knew something about me that I wouldn't discover for many more years.

How often, when you hear of something going differently from what your own beliefs dictate, do you respond with charged emotions of dismay ("How could/did that happen?"), or horror ("Oh, that's just terrible!"), or sympathy ("I'm sooooo sorry!"), rather than just taking in what you are hearing, making it neither right nor wrong? In our society, we habitually answer from the perspective of self-relating. In other words, when we hear of something termed "tragic," unconsciously our response comes from fear in relation to how we would feel if the same thing were to happen to us.

Yet when in retrospect, almost always (I actually want to simply say "always"), it can be seen that what was viewed as unwanted at the time has turned out to be its own blessing. It's not that we would willingly, if that were an option, bring the unwanted event forward, but rather, that the unforeseen perfection of it becomes obvious over time.

You may recall the woman I spoke of earlier, whom I gave a massage to when I was working as a volunteer at Hospice, and who was in her final stage of life. More often than not, the people I spoke with in Hospice, and like the woman I mention here again, expressed how cancer had been a gift—albeit an unwanted one—in that it had changed their relationship with people and life, bringing them into the place of cherishing everything just as it is, without the need to change it, and without expectations or demands.

Sometimes the blessing initially can look devastating. Our life-detours, as I mentioned earlier, can be short, given our knowing and awareness, or they can be longer and more tortuous if we are resisting where the soul wants to go. The latter was the case of someone I know well. He was academically well qualified to enter any discipline he wanted to, plus he was a good writer and a promising artist. However, rather than heeding the wisdom that some minor incidents could have given him, he decided to make his detour long and tortuous, filled with drugs and alcohol. Eventually he sank to the bottom of the pit when he became addicted to crack along with other drugs and alcohol. The gas was turned up to such a degree that it was no longer bearable to live with the pain he was carrying, it had become life or death, and he chose life. Whatever the forces were that came forward, he was graced with an inner strength. Although this particular detour for him was excruciating and dangerous, it appears to be one he no longer feels the need to explore. Through a good treatment plan and lots of support, he made it through his own raging fires of hell to the other side.

Through his challenging experiences, this man was able to be of service to so many people, all the while having the strength to come from tough love. He turned his experience into "How does this serve?" rather than taking the "Poor me, it's not my fault," route. He gave back to the community from his heart experience, which meant that others going through their hell could hear his story, and this often offered them the grasping straw that ultimately gave them the courage to face life. Although I myself might like to work with people battling addiction, I have no credibility; I haven't been there. We need people who have had their unique addiction experience, who are willing to speak about their story, who can explain and, more importantly, who can empathize with those caught in the snares of addiction. The same is true for any challenging experience; for example, for people who have been through the challenge of cancer. Survivors can turn what had once been their challenge into hope for others.

One New Year's Day many years ago, I woke up with the realization that I was going to quit smoking that day. To put this in perspective, I smoked at least a pack a day and, given certain situations that often occurred for me, such as two cocktail parties followed by more drinks, dinner, and after-dinner drinks all in the same evening, I could easily smoke two packs. Although even the thought is now repugnant, it was true for me at this stage of my life. I had tried quitting a number of times before, each attempt being short-lived. I even started playing a bit of a game with myself, telling myself every time I lit up how the cigarette was in charge of my life, how I was addicted to this stupid little white piece of paper. Then, seemingly out of nowhere, on this particular New Year's Day, when I awoke there was an inner voice as clear as any spoken one.

"Today you will quit smoking."

"Oh, no, no, no," said I, "I can't do that because I haven't had a smoke-out" (meaning smoking cigarette after cigarette until I felt I had had enough).

Then I bargained a bit. "Okay, I'll just have one last cigarette."

"You are not having another cigarette: you are quitting now."

Somehow, somewhere in me, I knew I was experiencing a window, an opportunity. I knew I needed to go through this or there would not be an opening again for a very long time, if ever. As I look back on that morning, I wonder what might have happened—how the gas might have been turned up for me—had I not listened to my inner voice. Would the next stage have been lung cancer?

The "what-ifs" are a struggle for many. "What if I had married John instead of Peter?" "What if I hadn't said such-and-such, would that have changed the way the relationship worked out?" "What if I hadn't taken Katie to school late that day, would the crash have happened?"

People write of the gift of their illness or the gift of the abuse they received early in life or the gift of desperation from being fired from their job. When we have the capacity to shift our perspective—to ask the question "How does this serve?"—we open ourselves to the ability to see the gift. People who have been told they have a limited time left find themselves truly living for the first time in their lives. People who have suffered abuse, when they shift in to compassion and self-awareness, see how the abuse shaped their character and made them survivors. Furthermore, they are able to help others in a way that someone without that experience cannot. People who have faced desperation, such as the loss of a job accompanied by the fear of financial ruin, find an inner strength that pulls them through and gives them a boost of fighting spirit. Often this leads to an opening to greater creativity in their lives, perhaps leading them into actually working in something that feeds their souls. Sometimes it takes that kind of shove from the gods to force us into doing what we have been unwilling to hear from our inner voice previously.

We can drive ourselves mad with these "what-ifs." Yet if we honestly look at our lives we can see the perfection of the what-ifs having been what they were. Turn this around and say, "I don't deal with what-ifs. Whatever happens, I'll deal with it."

Life appears to bring us what we need, offering opportunities for each of us to move forward in self-discovery, to move forward into freedom, to move into heaven on earth. It's when we take these opportunities and twist them through the distorting filters of our beliefs that they become "don't-wants" instead of gifts. This book is not about delving deep into the caves of the iceberg, that's more material for a class or individual session. Yet, perhaps, from giving some contemplative thought to situations you've been in, to your if-only-I-had-done-this thoughts, you will be able to see how what you did was perfect, leading you into the next meaningful person or situation in your life. This may include seeing how you chose certain detours, and perhaps this insight may even include seeing how the particular detour you're currently on has been long enough and that you are now ready to shift.

CHAPTER FOURTEEN:
The Truth About Freedom

Life, as we all know, is conflict, and man, being part of life, is himself an expression of conflict. If he recognizes the fact and accepts it, he is apt, despite the conflict, to know peace and to enjoy it. But to arrive at this end, which is only a beginning (for we haven't begun to live yet!), a man has got to learn the doctrine of acceptance, that is, of unconditional surrender, which is love.

Henry Miller, *The Wisdom of the Heart*

There's a perceived price to be paid for the freedom of living life from your truth. When I started contemplating what that price might have been for me, the question of marriage or no-marriage came up. It was an amazing moment when I realized that it is because of my no-marriage for the past many years that I have been free to be as spontaneous as I have been. My life since my last marriage has been very full, rich in experiences, exciting, and internally rewarding. I am enormously grateful that I have been able to drop everything and simply take off as the opportunities have arisen in front of me.

Being on my own is not something that would have ever crossed my mind. I have a vivid recall of myself in my early twenties when the thought, just the thought, of ever being of my own was terrifying to me. As I say this now, it is difficult to imagine, yet I do know that was how I felt at the time.

When I left my last marriage, it did not occur to me there was the slightest possibility I would not be in another committed relationship before long. Yet although it took me some time to come to the realization, I became aware, so many years after the end of this marriage, that my *not* being in any committed relationship has been an enormous gift and well worth the price. Learning to be okay with being alone, learning to enjoy my own company, learning to appreciate myself, learning to be okay in silence rather than meaningless chatter or background noise so as not to have silence, have all been invaluable. Being alone has given me my most intimate of all relationships—with myself and my Higher Self. Yes, I've had many experiences of abject loneliness, often accompanied with the laments of, as the song says, "Nobody loves me, everybody hates me, goin' down in the garden to eat worms." I had to learn that emotions were not going to kill me no matter how painful they may have felt at the time. Most importantly, I learned two significant things about myself. First, if I am *fully in the experience*—be it heartache, self-hate, fear, feeling invisible, or feeling unloved—when I fully experience the emotion, it morphs into a sense of calm and peace. Second, I myself create any suffering I am experiencing.

I have traveled a great deal in my life, for pleasure and for work, most often combining the two. I was blessed to eventually find a career I loved in energy medicine, teaching BodyTalk worldwide, and it often served as a jumping-off point for an adventure. Yet more times than I care to remember, friends would tell me they couldn't imagine traveling on their own. "How do you go to a restaurant on your own? Don't people stare at you?" My answer would be along the lines of "Well, what do you think my two choices are?" The choice really is either to travel alone or to stay at home, trapped by my own unwillingness to experience all that it means to be alone. Just because eating alone in a restaurant might feel uncomfortable, or wishing I had someone to share my travel experience with, was not reason enough for me to stay home. Each moment of dis-ease, being aware of what I was feeling instead of trying to stuff it down, allowed me to fully feel the discomfort and loneliness, thereby moving me into full enjoyment of where I was. Because I once so dreaded and feared being alone, that is exactly where life has had me sit.

Spontaneity seems to be a part of my nature, and being without a committed relationship has given me my spontaneous freedom, as in being free to make my decision without consulting a partner. When I feel called to do something, I generally do it. My last serious, and seriously dysfunctional, relationship was with someone who had not traveled nor was he very comfortable exploring anything out of his realm of familiarity. When I went to Bhutan with a couple of woman friends and a group, the trip acted as the catalyst for the end of this particular relationship. Bhutan was still an isolated country at the time, plus this was prior to the wide public use of cell phones and email—not that it would have mattered, because electronic communication was minimal in Bhutan. I was away for several weeks, and although I had explained I would not be in touch during this time, when I did call this man after I left Bhutan, I heard a distraught and angry person telling me how inconsiderate I had been to leave and I needed to come home right away. I had planned to continue for another week in Thailand with a friend, but I abandoned her to fend for herself there. I abandoned my good friend for a man and, sadly, I am not the first woman to do that. That was a barometer of the dysfunction of my relationship with this man.

Nevertheless, the end of this relationship was more painful than any other. I didn't understand at the time about being fully in an emotion, yet my grief did take me over. I was on my living room floor, near paralytic, for three days as grief consumed me. I didn't try to fight it. Once this episode was over and no grief was left, I was done. There was no desire in me to try and see him, to try and make things work. That was the gift of completion for having walked through the fire.

This man, and the man from the chapter *Don't Cry For Me Argentina*, my relationship before him, were both wonderful opportunities for me to dig deeply into the cavern of my unconscious, unveiling hidden pieces of my relationship self. There had been incredible connections for me with each of these men, as I've mentioned. I have just now, literally on writing these last couple of lines, become aware of something: that The Priest and The Dark Shaman triggered the same pattern as the other two men. If I were to add a minor difference, I would say that it was in the last two relationships that I began to notice myself more and, albeit at that point still mainly unconsciously, to notice the common pattern.

Some like to refer to profound connections with a partner as being with your soul mate and, at that time, I doubtless used that term myself. Each of these four men felt as though they were a continuation of my life from some other time, because they were so instantly familiar to me. I was so comfortable with feeling that I knew each of them in a deep way that was unrelated to having spent current time with them. Although writing this has brought up some discomfort from self-understanding, in that the memory alone reminds me of how stuck like in treacle I was at the time, I see as well how even the dysfunction of the pattern felt familiar—which would have been a good clue for me at the time had I been more self-aware. Feeling comfortable with a dysfunction is a common unconscious pattern prior to laying bare the pattern itself. To summarize mine with these men, I was caught in the place of giving myself away to be with men. Like many of us, I had father issues around love, and having the illusion of love felt nicer than not having it, so in this way I would diminish my own value and put theirs ahead of mine. In other words, I was living out a piece of "The Prostitute."

After my surrender into grieving that led to my letting go in the final relationship, I was able to be with myself on a new level. I was able to see the pattern. The gift was in seeing how I had been taken in, time after time, by the same unconscious pattern, thus showing me the internal work I needed to do with myself around it. These men were gifts, in their own unique ways, each one taking me deeper until I surrendered and, through the surrender, became more aware. I was also obsessively hooked by our connections. How could it be that they felt so familiar to me, and yet we were not together? It was a breakthrough for me when I was able to shift and see and own the unconscious patterns that had repeatedly hooked me into such obsessions, rather than actually needing to be together with someone.

As I looked more deeply, I began to see similarities among all my relationships. I had been indoctrinated by society into believing "I can't survive being alone." "Women don't live alone unless there's something wrong with them." "A woman isn't complete without a man." I had shoved down my own feelings. The men's feelings, wants, and needs were what mattered—they were more important than me.

Of course these are only pieces of who I was at that time, parts of my pathology hooked into certain beliefs around women, men, marriage, security, and so on. Only in retrospect was I able to see how I needed to learn to stand on my own two feet, to own wholly who I am and, later, better yet, who I am not. Then I could come into my own power.

I have a friend who has been married for over fifty years, nearly two-thirds of his lifetime. He feels enormously blessed with what is, for him, a wonderfully fulfilling life, his wife being central in it. A big piece of me envies that and yearns to have the same. Yet somehow I know, deep down, that if I had had that I wouldn't have been as willing to explore my dark caverns. Indeed, I may not have even entertained the idea.

My experience with couples in long-term relationships covers a range, from working with them professionally, to observing people in restaurants and at public events, to witnessing family and friends. The friend I mentioned above is, in my experience, a rare example of someone (who is seemingly) wholly content in, and grateful for, his relationship, even after so many years of commitment.

When I look around I see, energetically, what appears to be a great deal of suffering for people in relationships. Observing such couples is almost like reading a book about their pain. My memory now immediately takes me back to my own story, of being in a restaurant with my last husband and the tears pouring down my face uncontrollably. Even though the tears may be absent, it is the same energy I see so often in others, where the separation between two people is painfully obvious to me, if not to them.

Relationships have been for me, and most often are for others, one of the more challenging areas in spiritual maturation. It is said by many a spiritual teacher that an intimate relationship is our greatest life teacher. We tell little white lies rather than speaking from the heart about what we are feeling. More often than not, we say we don't want to hurt the other person, yet underneath it is that we don't want to take a risk. It feels as though there is a lot of risk in speaking our truth to our partner. Why is that? What are we risking?

"If I speak my truth, you may leave me." And the reality is that, yes, whenever we speak our truth we risk. So the mind says it is better to stuff it all down deep inside rather than be self-honest, living our own truth.

Many people stay in a relationship because of such fear of their partner leaving. "What's wrong with me that I couldn't make it work?" "How will I support myself financially?" (Frighteningly common for women yet also true for men who are being supported by their partner.) "I'm terrified of being on my own; I want someone to take care of me." Many men lament, "I can't possibly cook and change the bed, and I don't want to hire a housekeeper." "People will think something is wrong with me if I don't have a relationship." "I can't work full-time, pick up dry-cleaning, and cook dinner. I need someone to handle my life for me, to take care of me." (Like the financial fear for women, this is common for men.) The list goes on.

So when we lie—whether it's a little white lie, so that the other person doesn't know what we're honestly feeling, or a big fat lie—we are nevertheless suppressing a piece of ourselves. We are playing once again in the field of "The Prostitute" every time we dismiss, disown, or negate a piece of ourselves. We're choosing this over standing in our truth, yet the truth is stored energetically in the body. Eventually, over time, the energetic truth tends to have some physical manifestation in the body.

Interestingly, sexual dysfunction or lack of response can be one of these manifestations. I remember well a couple who were working on their relationship, which had gone dead for both of them. No sex and no interest in sex, from either, for years. The guy assumed he had erectile dysfunction and the woman assumed she had lost her interest in sex because of her belief around age-related change in hormones. And besides, she would have a dry vagina, wouldn't she? That would make sexual intercourse uncomfortable—that's what the experts said. Well, guess again. They decided to end the relationship, and before long they were both hot into new ones. No little blue pill was needed for the guy, and the woman had no difficulty responding in a warm juicy way. We have bought into a huge marketing lie around sexuality and response.

Religion is another area where we lie to ourselves big time. Indeed, religion itself is a lie, given that it is simply person after person parroting what they've been told by someone who has also not had their own experience. Thousands of years of parrots!

R&R: relationships and religion have this in common, just like everything else. We are chock-full of beliefs about how relationships are *supposed to be*: how the other person is *supposed* to behave, how we're *supposed* to spend all our time with our partner, and how we're *supposed* to be nice to our partner—whatever "nice" actually is. While members of a religion, we are told to believe what we are told, according to the doctrine of that particular denomination, without questioning how life is for us. Indeed, religion also often dictates beliefs about the "shoulds" and "thou shalt nots" of marriage.

The reality is that many marriages hang on not because the couple desires to be in the marriage any longer but because of fear of getting out, and the same is true of religion. In religion, there is the built-in conditioning that comes from having made God personal. We then put ourselves in the place of having to please God and play by "His" rules. Only the clincher is, God didn't hand out any rules—they are human-made but handed out as though they were God-made! (The Gnostic Gospels, considered to be the least altered texts from Jesus' time, do not, to the best of my knowledge, contain rules of a personal God.)

If we examine religions without prejudice, it becomes painfully obvious that all religion was created out of fear, the best dynamic for controlling the masses. The underlying created fear is, "If I don't do as the God of my religion dictates (by following all the rules) then (insert the fate of your choice) will happen."

Take the caste system in India: "If you don't surrender to your status of being the lowest of human beings, you will come back at an even lower stage." Or Catholicism: "If you don't go to confession and confess all of your sins, you will go to purgatory for a long time or maybe even to hell." Or Islam: "If you fail to obey your husband, you will be punished by torture or death." And look at the prayer that ultra Orthodox male Jews say every day: "Thank you, God, for not making me a woman."

A religion gets formed by men of certain beliefs, based on what they feel is their God-given message. Eventually, however, ideological disagreement and dissension develop, which lead to another person declaring that he has been given a message from God that says he's right and the founder of the religion is wrong.

How is it that we have come to make the Divine so small and personal that religion matters?

Interestingly, because relationships and religion are filled with strongly held beliefs, we also see strong areas of defense. How does our expression of our truth become our defense?

Being in our truth is about connecting with our own experience. What commonly happens, however, is that some people end up manipulating the emotional information and turning it into a slippery disguise. "I just need to tell you my truth," becomes a convenient way of dumping on the other person while using the words to make it appear as though you are telling them how you are feeling. Your feeling, hence your experience, belongs to you and not to the other person. It's about you noticing what *you* are feeling and responding to what is in front of you from that place. For example, you would turn around the above phrase and respond with something like: "I'm feeling furious right now. I'm feeling controlled and disconnected from you." This isn't reacting to the other person; rather, it's receiving what they have said or done and noticing that you are feeling angry. You are not making the other person responsible for your anger. You are owning that they and/or their action touched a button in you.

Another form of defense happens when we react and walk away from the other person without communicating what we are experiencing. "You made me feel… and therefore I am leaving you." Often this type of reaction is accompanied by some sort of statement about not wanting to continue the relationship, all the while pointing a blaming finger at the other person rather than owning our own feelings. The very discomfort that leads to the expression of not wanting the relationship ought to be an indicator of the suppressed button that has been pushed.

When we are in a relationship—whether it's an intimate partnership, an intimate friendship, or close family—if we respond as in the above-mentioned pointing-finger examples, we can be guaranteed one thing—that eventually the relationship will die. The unclaimed material, from all of the suppression of what was going on for you, will be stored. Unraveling all of the sticky guck will have become so thick that saving the relationship at this stage will be nigh on impossible. Conversely, richness in a relationship comes from being willing to listen to the other person, to notice *our* reactions and defenses, to take responsibility for our rising emotion, and to respond to the other from that place.

No one can make you feel something! End of story. I realize this can be difficult to grasp, especially because we have become so conditioned to saying "You made me feel thus and so," or "How could you do this to me?" We do not like to let go of our illusion that, "This is your fault." Whether we want to delve deeper or not, life is using such experiences to stir our inner pot, to force a breakthrough into a deeper self-understanding. We don't have to go there—we can take another of our avoidance detours if we prefer—but it seems that eventually life will kick our butt in one form or another to drop us smack into the muck.

Spiritually mature people own that they are responsible for what they are feeling. From that place, they will no longer dump on others. Having a disagreement with someone will then lead to our own introspection rather than taking it out on the other person in blame. Once this happens, your life path will feel smooth and gently curving rather than tortuous.

CHAPTER FIFTEEN:

Secrets, Anyone?

The man who can keep a secret may be wise, but he is not half as wise as the man with no secrets to keep.

Edgar Watson Howe

Secrets are interesting and they come with many disguises. We tend to think of them in a specific way, such as hiding something about ourselves that we absolutely don't want anyone to know. But there are other, more sneaky kinds of secrets.

When we hold on to a secret, what is it saying about us? Why does it seem so seriously important that we keep these pieces hidden, lest others find out about them? Isn't it really that we do not embrace our full humanness? Also, in our arrogance, we think we're the only person who has ever had such deeds or thoughts that cannot be exposed.

It's always a revealing time when a person participating in a group shares a secret. First, it's really not a big deal. Honestly. The person discovers that no one really cares about your secret, and, more importantly, that even if others don't have the same secret, they can nevertheless always relate to yours on some level.

The point around resistance is that we do not want to own shadow aspects of ourselves. As an example, there was a participant in one of my groups who likes to stay in what I call "the love, light, and harmony" place. She described herself as being a kind, nice, positive, helpful, and supportive person, and she wanted to talk about a "very negative" woman that she works with who has been "pushing her buttons." As we went deeper into self-exploration for her, however, some of the participants offered feedback to help her see the other pole of her (and therefore their) "positive" pieces. On hearing some descriptive words—such as mean, negative, controlling, manipulative—about herself from the opposite pole to the love, light, and harmony pieces, her resistance rose up like a cobra, guarding the inner door with angry denial. The sheer thought of acknowledging in any way that these pieces were also a part of her wholeness created a deeper burrowing into these secret cavities where the denial pieces needed to stay hidden. She had such a frantic desire to keep the shadow pieces hidden from everyone's view and, most importantly, from herself. It was devastating to her to imagine people seeing these unclaimed aspects, given that she had spent her entire life working on being a positive, happy, and very, *very* nice person.

To own the dual nature of self can be tantamount to letting out the biggest secret of our life. Yet releasing resistance to our wholeness is a key to our well-being. Becoming familiar with all we are is also the key to freedom. I love my bitch, for example. I know I can be as nasty as I can be loving. I know I can be a victim and feel sorry for myself, and also that if you put a victim in front of me I can become a victimizer in a nanosecond. By having made friends with the unflattering, unsavory pieces of myself, I am accepting of all of me. Even if I might choke on discovering something that I'm just bringing into my conscious awareness, I am nevertheless committed to claiming all of me, which means accepting that, yes, these are also parts of me. Most importantly, the now-familiar pieces don't sneak up out of the dark shadows to create havoc in my life.

I do want to mention that there can be some misunderstanding if people explore the shadow side of their being on their own. The ego can grab hold of this process and manipulate the shadow piece in such a way that the mind convinces someone that this may be true for others, but not for them. In this way the exploration can become a deterrent to self-understanding rather than an opening. The ego is slippery and does not want to be revealed, because it knows that once discovered, its power is lost, or at least greatly diminished. In trying to remain powerful, the mind will argue and deny. In the above case, for example, the need to protect the unsavory, undesirable aspects of self was so strong that the woman declared I was "abusing" her and "yelling" at her. The other participants, however, had directly opposite points of view from hers. This serves as an important reminder that the place for exploring "The Shadow" needs to be done with the realization that none of this is personal; everyone has the other pole of whichever trait one wants to name—hence the need for a sincere willingness to do "whatever it takes" to break through resistance into acceptance. In this specific case, I misinterpreted this woman's level of self-understanding. Had I read her more clearly, I would have left her in her own defense, as she was not at the point of willingness to go through the door that shakes us open.

Owning the shadow pieces does not mean acting them out. Rather, it requires noticing when the shadow piece shows up. From that noticing, the energy tends to dissipate. It's simply an acknowledgement of, "Yes, I am that, too" or, in noticing it in another person, acknowledging the piece of "just like me."

Continuing with the case I mentioned, this same woman did, however, break through, and she cried for three days. I was very pleased to hear of her crying, because from my experience this indicated there was a lot of movement happening. A few days later she was able to slowly see how her defenses had kept her from owning the "not so nice," "negative" bits of herself. So, as always, I just trust the process, even though I learned an important piece for myself. I expect I will see this woman again in another group, when next I am in her area. As the Buddhists say, once the door is opened, it cannot be closed again.

Often, if young children express a shadow aspect of themselves, parents react in a horrified manner that their child would say such a thing. Then the children learn to be horrified about such aspects, too. I recall a male client telling me how, even as a young child, he thought he was evil, the devil incarnate, because of the "bad" thoughts he had. This became a deep dark secret to never tell anyone, contributing to making him feel unworthy, with low self-esteem. He wouldn't tell his parents of his feelings because of guilt of how his revealing these pieces of himself would make them feel. "How could our beautiful child, who we have been teaching to be nice and good and kind, have such dreadful thoughts? How could you?" The answer is simply because they themselves were denying the same pieces within themselves.

Often secrets from childhood involve sexuality. Many boys, for example, experiment with sex in a number of ways, by themselves or with others. The "ways" do not matter; what does matter is if there is guilt and shame as a result. This translated out for this particular male client to feelings of sexual inadequacy in his adult life, coupled with a continuing sense of low self-esteem. How could he be such a bad, evil person? In this fellow's case, when he revealed the deep secret he had held on to so tightly to a therapist, it was an enormous relief for him that the therapist not only had no judgment around his revelations but had also heard it all before. As with any secret, we think it is ours alone to carry, never anyone else's before.

Sexual issues can also be common secrets for girls. Although this is not the place to discuss the collective aspects of sexuality, these are nevertheless huge pieces within our psyche, whether we are male or female. The big, deep, dark, horrible, unforgivable secret that some women hold is around having been sexually abused and, on some level, enjoying it. What was "wrong" with them that they could enjoy something that everyone knows is horrible and dirty?

A big part of the reason we hold on to secrets is that we fall into the trap of believing there is a personal right and wrong, a good and a bad. We are human beings living in our dualist Universe, hence the polarity of, for example, right and wrong. (This is not addressing the Universal Law, which is impersonal, absolute, and therefore non-dualistic.)

Again, have you thought about what it means to call someone "bad" or to declare some action as "wrong"? Remember, as with all beliefs, the questioning has to start with "and who said so?" Although it's astonishingly simple, we most often don't question. If I say, for example, that someone is wrong, the person who is being referred to will (more than likely) respond defensively that I am the one who is wrong and they are the one who is right. That's what creates the polarity. By virtue of human beings declaring that they think they know something, when the reality is that we really know nothing, a "right" has been established. Given that there is now a label called "right," there has to be an opposing label called "wrong," regardless of what is being labeled. The right/wrong are established based on personal beliefs.

Although we, as egoic human beings, like to think that our thoughts have never existed before, in the hologram of existence all potential exists within all of us. Therefore you cannot have an "evil" thought that has never been thought before. Besides, where do you your thoughts come from, anyway? When you can answer that, you'll win the prize, because in truth, no one knows. People may have their theories, but no one *knows*. Thoughts happen. Period. We say, "It popped into my head," which appears to be accurate. We don't intend to think an "evil" or "bad" thought, it just happens. The important, revealing catch, however, is that it's the *thinking* that comes after the thought that then creates the resistance, judgment and the reaction. So going back to right/wrong, good/bad, we have seen that it is *only* our beliefs that make something right or wrong. A thought happens. It pops into our head, we say, without our participation. The thought itself is neither good nor bad; it is simply a thought that has been thought before. Nothing original. As a person deepens their understanding of the thought being simply a thought without a label, the mind quiets and the mind chatter becomes dramatically reduced. The thoughts then just flow in, are noticed, and flow out. However, when the mind grabs a thought, based on unconscious and perhaps conscious beliefs around the thought, and thinking happens after the thought, that then becomes another matter entirely. Once the mind has latched on to the thought, the flow of our conditioned beliefs begins to label the thoughts. "Something must be wrong with me because I have these terrible thoughts. I know I'm no good; no good person could think like me."

The resistance to, in this case the secret of "bad" thoughts, is where the charge hangs out. We've labeled the thought as "bad" and we do not want anyone to know what a horrible person we are. So we shove the thought deep down and hold it as our very own little secret. Little do we know just how common and ordinary our thoughts are. Move through the resistance by balancing the duality. Through claiming the unwanted thought along with the preferred thought so that we can see them both as the same, without a charge or preference, we will feel free.

You may recall the story of my mother and the big secret she held on to for so many years about her younger sister having been raped, the subsequent pregnancy, and the adoption of the child. When my mother called to let me know about this niece contacting her so many years later, she ended the story by telling me how her huge secret burden had been lifted from her. In esoteric terms, her heart had become less veiled. Her heart was lighter, she felt lighter. What a wonderful gift for her to have had this release rather than dying holding on to the secret. My cousin Maxine, the niece whom my mother had never met before, was also given a great gift when she released her resistance to finding her mother. Through so many years she had held on to her story that her mother had not wanted her and willfully abandoned her. When it was time for her to release her resentment and bitterness, life showed her how false her story had been.

Our mind manipulates thoughts to protect the personal shadow; hence our unconscious manipulation can also be a slippery way for an undesirable piece to remain hidden. For example, someone might say that they "intuitively know" something or use the phrase "my truth is…" to actually keep a secret. The mind is so clever and tricky that the person will be thoroughly convinced that they have had a great insight. People often see themselves as "enlightened" in that they are speaking from their "truth" when it's actually "The Shadow" being covered with another layer of camouflage. Using these deflective phrases, albeit probably unconsciously, effectively cuts off the path to revealing something that would, in their belief, make them appear less "enlightened." "Phew! Another secret that had managed to escape detection!"

There can be other less obvious secrets, yet they are secrets nonetheless. Many like to say they are "private" people who "don't want everyone to know my business," as though it actually matters. It only matters to the person holding the secret. And what does "being a private person" actually say about that person? From my perspective, they are really saying they don't want you to know them. This immediately limits the kind of relationship I can have with this person, because they've basically told me they want to remain superficial. They have pieces of themselves that they do not want me to know. Yet the juicy bit of life is when someone gives me something of themselves. I immediately become engaged. I am open to the person, without judgment, just there to receive what they are choosing to tell me. I know from my own experiences of when I do the same and share something very personal, how this connects me with the other. It doesn't matter what it is I am sharing; it could be something commonplace or something revealing about myself. The point is that when we share a piece of ourselves with another, a connection is made. That comes from my knowing there is nothing I have that needs to be kept hidden.

I was in an airport sitting in a restaurant waiting for a flight. A woman came by my table and we recognized each other because we had exchanged a couple of comments when we were shopping in the same store. She joined me and after a few minutes of travel talk she said something that led me into telling her a piece of my life and about a particular struggle. This opened her up to tell me about her daughter who had committed suicide. We had gone in a very short time from two strangers, to intimate human beings having a spiritual experience. All it takes is for you to be willing to be totally seen while being openly honest about yourself, and you will experience that the illusion of separation dissolves immediately. You will see the other as you and the other will see you as them. It's an experience of Oneness; it is an awakening moment.

Another form of keeping secrets is the way in which many people handle their personal relationships. By this I mean deliberately keeping people in their lives separate so that often one friend knows nothing about another friend, even though they may each be considered "very close friends."

So that it may be easier to see how this could play out, I will relay a situation of a female client who was insanely jealous of her lover. The jealousy translated out to possessiveness plus not wanting her partner to have an opportunity to hear anything about her past from an intimate female friend of hers who just might reveal some of her little self-flattering white lies. Given that her lover actually liked the other woman as a person, the only way to prevent any such conversation from happening, while at the same time refusing to claim her jealousy, was for her to end this long-term intimate friendship under the guise of "not feeling connected any longer." We could also say that this is another good example of a woman selling herself out for a partner.

Knowing the circumstances and those involved, the honest approach would have been for the woman to claim her jealousy. "I need to end our friendship because my relationship with my partner is more important to me than you. I'm jealous of you, and I don't want to risk that in time my jealousy could come out in our relationship and have a detrimental effect." Now, that would have been honest, and the energy would have been clean around it.

When we want to control the unfolding, as in these examples, we fall into the illusion of believing we are actually going to steer life to give us what we desire. My experience, however, shows that when we deny our secrets or what we view as our unsavory pieces—such as lies, jealousy, fear of discovery, rejection—the detour will result in giving us just what we don't want. In the second example, it would not surprise me to see the lover leave this woman.

Jealousy itself is nothing more than fear of losing the "hold" on the other person. Ironically, when there are no secrets and no need to exaggerate or tell our little white lies, there is no need for jealousy. Transparency with a partner is an intimacy that is, of itself, a strong bond. It goes along with the understanding that you are there with this person in your life at this moment, and myriad things could happen to change that. The only value is in being *fully* in the relationship in the moment.

Following through on the above examples, it is rather common to see people wanting to keep their lives fragmented and separate so that one person knows only certain aspects or experiences of the friend while another may know totally different pieces. Again, is it because of the fear of being revealed in some way? Of lies being exposed? Is it because of a possessiveness to keep friends from meeting each other, perhaps for fear of a connection between the friends? Or is it the illusion that you would lose your friendships if everyone knew everyone else?

"Did you see a movie on the weekend?"

"Yes."

Here is some hesitation about sharing with someone who is supposed to be a good friend. It's like a closed door. Open friendship might mean saying something like, "Yes, I went to such-and-such movie with my friend Mary."

When I am faced with people who want to keep their life to themselves, I find I eventually get to the place where I no longer want to share much with the person and the friendship begins to wane. Putting up your guard about sharing your activities is a blatant example. Seriously, if you're talking to a friend, what is behind the need to be so guarded?

Let me contrast this with a close friend of mine who is a therapist. We appreciate our friendship because of our mutual willingness to be totally seen by the other. She was expressing to me, while I was writing this chapter, how she had come to acceptance of the piece of herself that feels scared over a seemingly small thing. Previously she had denied this in herself because, after all, as a highly qualified psychotherapist, shouldn't she know better? As she was working with a therapist around this scared piece, she remembered this feeling from an incident with her father when she was young that related to money. What she had been doing since then was denying how scared she was whenever she was faced with anything around personal finances. Following this acceptance she now just allows, "I'm feeling scared and I'm okay with feeling scared." No explanation needed.

When someone gives me an intimate piece of themselves, like how this friend did, I immediately feel open and loving toward the person. This is what I need, not secrets. Share with me your life, and I will be an open book for you. I seek intimacy, I yearn for intimacy, because this is the space where we can connect. How can we have intimacy with our friends if our secret door is so closely guarded? I imagine Robin Williams would agree with me here about intimacy. His poignant way of describing this for himself was when he said, "I used to think the worst thing in life was to end up all alone. It's not. The worst thing in life is to end up with people that make you feel all alone."

CHAPTER SIXTEEN:

Dying is a One-Man Show

The seeker should not stop until he finds. When he does find, he will be disturbed. After being disturbed, he will be astonished. Then he will reign over everything.

These words, said by Jesus, open the great Gospel of Thomas

To see a world in a grain of sand

and a Heaven in a wild flower,

Hold Infinity in the palm of your hand

And Eternity in an hour.

William Blake

It is in emptying, in letting go, that one is most likely to encounter the Transcendent's revelatory mysteries and its resources. It is when we are most vulnerable and powerless that the psyche begins to make contact, and the Transcendent begins to make itself known as a guiding principle. It is an extraordinarily difficult time period, but this is like a long vision quest. You sacrifice all the usual things that have pleasured you, and protected you, and contained you, and when you sacrifice that energy to this most Transcendent process, it sacrifices something of itself to you—that is the mystery of this process.

There may not be intensity, epiphanies, or theophanies—it may all of a sudden get down to very simple things that one starts to experience. We don't have a burning bush every day…. Many people can never quite capture the understanding of the dynamism that it is in the vulnerability, and not in the power levels of the psyche, that we are truly taught that there is no resource within the personal range that is going to transform a situation—we have to be open to the Transcendent coming in.

Transformation occurs through vulnerability, in those areas where you feel most inadequate. To come to wholeness, you have to leave the comfort. The surface mind perceives this as something terrible. Nonetheless, impulses seek development and will overthrow that which is developed; you are cast into the undeveloped, unfulfilled. Historically, the cast-off mystery has served to disguise the hero for a while until he developed resources. Energy withdraws from what has been transformed and evolved—the manna is in the untransformed.

When something disappears from our life, the energy will come forth in a different way, at an equal or greater magnitude—it will just flow in. 'Oh, this is going, and what will be coming in?' instead of fixating on the loss and trying to get that back again; even if you could get it back, you'd end up holding the short end of the horn of Cornucopia. The psyche feels loss and it begins to bring in a resource out of that vulnerability. There are forces behind us that are supporting us and connect us to greater possibility.

If one's heart is genuine, all of the concerns, all of the fears, all is redeemed at a later point in time, and then there's a Presence that sees much more deeply and no longer gets hooked into the same older patterns.

Brugh Joy

I am taking the liberty to use several powerful quotes to open this chapter in my final attempt to grab your attention. I want to remind you that life is not a dress rehearsal and that dying is truly a one-man show. If it is in your cards to experience the dying process, you will realize that you and only you are in the deathbed. If I am given the opportunity to know I am in transition, I do not want to be dying with regret that I lived my life for others by adhering to their beliefs of "have-tos" and "shoulds." Nor do I want to realize any lost opportunities of saying "yes" before "no" or of being able to tell those significant in my life my truth. As I have seen at various times in Hospice, when the light goes on and the person sees how they have lived their life for others, not for themselves, it is truly heartbreaking. Yet at that time it is too late to do anything with that realization. This is a detour I feel I am avoiding, at least to a large degree, and it is what spurs me on to live my life as fully as I can until my expiration date.

There is magic everywhere. Your task is to pay attention, notice the magic, drop into astonishment, and feel the Grace that is guiding you in your life.

See the Divine in an old woman's face that opens your heart; feel the pure love of a child's tiny hand holding yours. Hear the Divine in Mozart who knew he was not the creator of the music. In the succulent huckleberry you were gifted to find, taste the Divine. The smell of a fragrant rose, long a symbol of love, offers itself in love. There is nothing complicated about the Divine. All that is required is for you to give your attention to what is in front of you.

A friend of mine recently died from pancreatic cancer. Although she and I had been good friends during a time when we were attending a lot of workshops together, our paths then took us in different directions. We would see each other on occasion, have a warm sharing chat, and then not be in touch until another spontaneous event brought us together.

On one such chance happening, I could see my friend had lost a great deal of weight that, she explained, was due to having been diagnosed with diabetes. This time, when we parted, we agreed to get together for a longer visit over coffee, which we did do.

Shortly after this visit she called and asked me to come and see her. It was then she told me she had just been diagnosed with pancreatic cancer. She had been given an appointment to see a surgeon, to discuss her options in addressing the cancer, and she asked if I would take her. In some cases, surgery for pancreatic cancer is a high-risk possibility, and in her cancer, surgery was not even in the realm of possibility. The statistics on having chemotherapy or radiation were also not encouraging. Although she had been concerned about what decision she would take, she now felt relief as there was no decision to make.

She then asked me if I would help her through this journey, which I was honored to do. Her desire to remain at home was deeply touching to me, as I instantly related to how, for me, that would also be my wish, given such a situation. Although I had never approached anyone's health crisis in this way before, I could immediately see how the daily simple tasks of life were now challenges all on their own to her. To deal with this, I organized a team of friends as volunteers for her care, two to come in every morning. Such a simple thing, really, yet this made such a difference to everyone involved. Friends felt as though they were actually helping out, while my friend was enormously grateful for all this. Within a very short time, the need for this help expanded to include helping her shower, putting cream on her body, straightening her bed, doing the laundry, and whatever else.

I went over to see her every afternoon—for our personal visit as well as to see if there were any specific things she needed, any preference for certain volunteers coming at certain times and the like. Our chats often included the subject of death and dying, as well as the practical aspect of dying, such as what she needed to take care of legally, how she wanted her funeral, and so on. Then on one day, not too far from her leaving, on a bright winter day, a beam of light came through her large bedroom window, shining on the wall where my friend could see it. It formed the shape of a heart. No other facets of light, just the heart.

For me, the magic of the heart beaming onto the wall was awesome. My comment to her, which sums up how I saw it, was: "Short of you getting a hand-written message from God, this is about as good as it gets!"

A few days later she was being transferred to Hospice. It was snowing heavily as the medics were getting her out to the ambulance on the stretcher. With a smile she said, "I just love feeling the snowflakes on my face!" She was totally in her experience of the moment. There was no dying, no leaving her home for hospice; there were only the crystalline snowflakes as they landed on her skin. When she got there, she was thrilled that her room had large windows looking out on to the trees, whose branches were now sagging under the weight of the snow. This was one of her last sights on this physical plane.

Thanks to a group of friends who wanted her to know they cared, my friend only had one and a half days in Hospice before passing.

Being witness to a friend who is transitioning out of this life is a gift. If you are given this opportunity, take it. Organize volunteers for your friends so that they can remain in the comfort of their home for as long as possible. This allows for a conscious passing. Soft music playing, perhaps, and candles if desired. Holding a hand, lightly stroking an arm or the face, or holding someone can bring a connection many have never experienced. Professionals can come in to handle the medical stuff from the physical perspective; it's the personal connection that comforts the spirit.

Like my friend, are you willing to put all of your energy on what is in front of you? Can you feel the warmth of the sun on your face? Can you look someone in the eye, from your heart? Can you savor the kiss of a person dear to you, or have you become complacent about a kiss? Could you ever walk out the door with the awareness this might be the last time you see this person?

Remember the woman I spoke of who was dying of lung cancer when I was working at Hospice? It was the touch of my hands as I massaged her back that dropped her into the realization that she had actually never felt a human touch until then. Her sorrowful wailing from deep within her expressed the sadness of what she had missed.

Touch is the most important of all of our senses; human beings cannot live without touch. Yet how many times have you not truly felt, as in openly receiving, someone's warmth and touch when it was waiting for you? When someone was there, when you had opportunities to ask that someone caress, massage, or touch you with heart-hands, what kept you from asking for what you were so deeply yearning? What keeps us from initiating authentic heart communication? Owning our own sense of vulnerability and yearning can quickly turn our defense against our deep feelings into receiving what we are most seeking. "He touched me," can mean both physically being touched as well as being touched in the Heart. Hopefully, we will all be able to fully take in the touch of another before we reach our expiration date.

Brugh Joy would often say, "There can be no transformation without crisis." It does seem that often crisis is the needed catalyst to give us an extra big push. One such crisis can be pain. Constant continuous pain can drop a person into the "now" better than most things. If the person is available to their process, the pain becomes the gift into a breakthrough of understanding.

So while we seem to have preferences for avoiding discomfort and certainly pain, if we pay attention, we can find the gift in the pain.

Throughout these chapters, I've mentioned the paradox of the simplicity and the difficulty of hearing our internal messages. We all receive messages; sometimes we hear them and sometimes it seems we are unconscious, unaware of them. Yet even when we do hear them, we often fail to act on them. We tend to give more trust to the external than to these voices of our Higher Self.

Intuition is available to everyone; no one is more intuitive than another. Learning to act on our internal message, however, without the mind interfering and arguing the opposite, comes from practice. It's like using a muscle—the more you use it, the stronger it becomes. In very short order, you learn to trust your intuition, and when you get the intuitive hit, as I call it, you act. "Go and see (a friend)," and you go without saying to yourself why you haven't the time. "Don't eat that." And you don't eat it. "Go there." And you make plans to attend. (As I mentioned earlier, however, the mind is such a slippery thing that we also need discipline while learning the difference between intuition and the shadow burrowing deeper into the cave. After responding to our intuition, a major dose of self-honesty can be helpful, checking to see whether we are using it to get what our ego says we want.)

Certainly, if we are willing to explore our beliefs, if we're willing to dig deep and pull them out of their hiding places, our ability to tune into our intuition increases. We get cloudy when we have judgments about this and that, so that what was initially an intuitive hit gets morphed by our unconscious beliefs into a mind-driven decision.

I have given many stories to illustrate the magic unfolding of our lives. When we look back in review, we see how it appears as though we each have our life-script. We see how people have come into our lives in ways we could not have created, to participate in some way in our life-movie. Some seem to be long-term participants in our life journey—such as my dear friend and ally of so many years who came into my life through my last marriage—while others may wax and wane, in and out of our lives at various times. Still, others seem to fade into the background of our stage, not discarded in any way, just no longer an active participant. If you are in my life-movie, then it would appear I am also in yours. It seems we play out various scenes with each other, dependent on our beliefs.

A friend went to visit her mother in a town an hour away and took her out to a restaurant for dinner. The waitress was an engaging young woman who, as a student, was only working part-time, although this night she was there and assigned my friend's table. Everyone exchanged pleasantries, and as my friend was paying the bill the waitress asked if she were single, to which she replied that she was. The waitress remarked: "My dad is the nicest man; I think you would really like him. Could I please give you his email?" That was the beginning of the closest relationship this friend of mine has had in her life. "He is my best friend!" The synchronicities that accompany their story are truly wonderful reminders, yet again, of how we could not create our life-scripts. Yet, if we are willing to be open to all possibility in acknowledging the unfolding of life, magic happens.

Whenever I make someone or something wrong, I remember (albeit at times a bit delayed) to bring myself back to the realization that my making the other person wrong is the other's right, regardless of the situation. I admit it's not always easy for me to dig deep enough to come to that realization within myself. As an example, if we look at a more charged situation and ask ourselves what makes a terrorist, we are still in the place of right and wrong. How do you think terrorists become terrorists in the first place? Years ago, before terrorism was an oft-spoken word, a young man became a world-famous terrorist when he kidnapped a group of high-powered men. He wasn't after personal money; he was after what he viewed as economic justice for the people of his country. When the suppressed stand up to the suppressor, who then is the terrorist?

Our perception of our personal reality is based on our beliefs. As the wonderful saying goes, "When we change the way we look at things, the things we look at change." It's not that anything "out there" changes. Rather, it is that "in here" shifts through understanding to see how we are the creators of our reality through our beliefs.

I realize each of you reading this have your own perceptions of how you live your life, and certainly your own priorities. I trust that life will bring each of us what we need, while our unique task is to have the courage to be with what is in front of us at the moment. If our priority is otherwise and we want to avoid what is put in front of us, what life is asking of us, we will take a detour. The detour can be tortuous, long, and repetitive; or, if we are courageous enough to choose to become more self-aware, the detour can be shortened as we gain insight into a particular pattern and eventually put it to rest.

I wish you increasing awareness to shorten your detours.

Some people I know seem to have been given an extra chance at life. It's like my mother having been given the three months and three weeks that, according to the specialists, she would not have. From my perspective, it seems that the hand of the Divine—also known in my language as *it just so happened*—plucks the person from the door of death and gives them another opportunity for self-understanding. A woman I met was an owner, along with her husband, of several restaurants. It *just so happened* that she was working one evening at this one particular restaurant of theirs when she quite literally dropped dead. Two nurses from ER *just happened* to be having dinner there and were able to bring her back by using CPR. Interestingly, the cardiac workup later showed no sign of heart disease and indeed could offer no explanation for what had happened. The experience, however, changed the life of the woman and of her husband. They changed their diets dramatically and offered many more healthy choices on their restaurant menus. They also chose to look more closely at how they lived their lives.

Over many years of observing people, myself included, and through my work, I have seen how the releasing of the illusions behind the beliefs that we hold to be true results in a shift in our vibration that translates out to a physical lightening in our body. It's like the burden of the secret my mother carried, which, when she released it, lifted a huge energetic weight off her. So it is for any of us if we are willing to self-explore. It is through this process that we release energies from our inner caverns, where they have been holding what is akin to a chunk of cement, blocking the pathways of our energies, which want to flow freely up and down our body's meridians.

I wish you the courage and the willingness to self-explore.

I wish you wellness in your physical, emotional, and spiritual bodies.

I know from my life experiences that the dismantling of strongly held-on-to beliefs translates out to a freedom of energy. Being free of the burdening chains means that you have increased energy to be in life, fully. This in turn manifests in a vibrancy and vitality of spirit, a strong gait, a youthfulness, and an energy that others are drawn to. When we are unburdened by useless beliefs, our body functions differently because of the free flowing energy. We are, after all, simply dense energetic bodies that appear solid.

As we get to know ourselves, the need for an argument with anyone becomes less and less. The story gets revealed quickly, the right/wrong finally seems useless, along with the realization that an argument can never be won—one position from one person and a different position from the other. I had to smile because as I was writing this chapter, I heard a new statistic saying that people who argue frequently have a considerably shorter life span. So there's another good reason to get to know yourself intimately!

If you are facing a health challenge, or if someone in your life is, try to bring yourself back to the realization that the one common denominator we all have is that we are going to physically die to this body. *Everyone dies; not everyone lives.* Regardless of whether or not you have a health challenge, neither you nor I know how or when our expiration date will be reached. An illness does not mean you will die from it. You may and you may not. It's truly that simple. So my perspective is to not waste your energy of today on a tomorrow that never comes.

Be proactive in your life and do your part in choosing to live healthily. For the sake of your children and grandchildren's future, please help protect our Earth for the future by choosing to eat organically, avoiding at all cost any and all GMO foods (which eating organically certainly helps to eliminate), and using your voice to stop GMO. This is truly one of the most pressing problems on our planet today. Exercise daily, commune with nature—drawing energy from it—and be committed to living your truth. These actions will all help to give you a full existence until the curtain closing of your last act.

I imagine that most people, when asked about finding inner peace and calm in the midst of chaos, would say they seek such a state. Sri Anandagiriji is an extraordinarily beautiful human being whom I've had the pleasure of sitting with on various occasions. When he answers a question, his clarity slices through all of the beliefs. No matter what he says, there is no way to disagree, because his answer is so crystalline; there is no "perhaps" to hook on to. I hear truth in his answers. Here are examples of what he has to say about inner peace:

Inner peace begins the moment you choose not to allow another person or event to control your emotions.

Inner peace is never about how ugly or beautiful your thoughts are. Peace is about how comfortable you are with your thoughts.

Is it necessary that one has to end thought in order to find peace? Or is it possible that you find peace if you stop battling with your thoughts?

Sri Anandagiriji

If you are closing this book with even a touch of a feeling of being okay with life just as it is, without the need of wanting it any other way than the way it is just now, with no right or wrong or good or bad or positive or negative, then I feel I will have been of service to you in some small way. But don't be hard on yourself about judging. We all have our degrees of judgment. As we become more aware, we more quickly notice our judgment as it comes forward. In the noticing, watch as the energy of it dissipates. Remembering to say: "Just like me!" is a great tool for this. Make a sticky note and put it on your bathroom mirror.

Remind yourself that, in the personal realm, the only right or wrong or good or bad comes from the persistence of duality constructed by our beliefs. (This is not the same as the universal realm, which is not governed by the duality of our universe.)

May you be willing to self-examine whenever your projection makes something more than what it is, whether that be the "bad" pole or the "wonderful" pole; both are decisive. Rather, just allow whatever to be as it is.

May you allow the Such-ness or Is-ness of life; may you simply allow the experience without the need to label it.

I wish you inner sight to see the magic unfolding in front of you; I wish you the ear of hearing of that which is unspoken; I wish you the tasting of the deliciousness of life itself, of today; I wish you the smelling of the rain, the damp earth, and babies' skin; and most of all, I wish you openness to receive another's touch while touching their heart with your heart.

Thank you for being a part of my journey.

Namaste: the Divine in me honors the Divine in you.

There is nothing to practice. To know yourself, be yourself. To be yourself, stop imagining yourself to be this or that. Just be. Let your true nature emerge. Don't disturb your mind with seeking.

Nisargadatta Maharaj

In cosmic consciousness the psyche or individual consciousness expands to a cosmic or universal level. The small personality with its identification with the body, the mind, and relationships makes a radical shift so that the self now identifies with the non-local, timeless existence of the cosmos. So it is called cosmic consciousness.

Deepak Chopra

I'm no longer searching

just opening,

no longer trying to make sense of pain

but trying to be a soft and sturdy home

in which real things can land.

Mark Nepo

ACKNOWLEDGMENTS

It is with enormous gratitude and deep appreciation that I thank each and every person who has been a part of my life journey. No names are necessary, for if you have been in my life-movie, I have been in yours. For all the button pushing, mirroring, cause for self-reflection, and your willingness to participate, I THANK YOU.

To TFJ and MTJ,
know you have kept me here.

To LIJ,
thank you for the two most precious pieces of my life.

To MEJ and ATJ,
your beautiful open hearts have opened mine and
you are my life gifts. This is my gift to you.

Thank you to each of you, friends and professionals, for helping me in the many various ways it took to get this book published.

BOOK CLUBS

Several people have brought forward the idea of having discussion groups based on this book. For example, it has been said this is perfect for BOOK CLUBS. If you belong to a book club, or if you are an individual and you are interested in participating in online discussion sessions with the author, please go to www.newparadigmhealth.com for further information.

Click on "Book" in the left-hand column. This will take you into specific information for online discussions with the author, both privately for individuals as well as for group sessions.

If you are interested in forming a group in your area and would like the author there to do a two-day gathering, please contact her by email at: beverly@newparadigmhealth.com

DISCUSSION QUESTIONS

Following are some sample questions that you may use for book clubs or in discussion with the author. These are put forward simply as suggestions. Individual questions can be submitted.

1: If you could choose to control everything in your life, what would that look like for you?

2: Are you aware of pieces of yourself that you want to keep hidden from others?

3: What are some things that are you holding on to that have been done to you by individuals or society, or how are you suffering because of your role as the offender in someone else's life?

4: How do you define freedom?

5: What are your biggest regrets?

6: Do you come from a religious paradigm? How has that served you?

7: What life role/roles do you identify with? (e.g. mother, father, son, daughter, martyr)

8: What are your feelings and/or fears around aging and dying?

9: What is your deepest secret?

10: Who can't you forgive? How has this influenced your life?

11: Who cannot forgive you? How has this influenced your life?

12: What does forgiveness look like for you?

13: What do you resist most about yourself? What parts do you deny?

14: What is your story?

15: What are your main detours and the patterns you continually repeat throughout your life?

16: Where do your beliefs come from?

17: Do you mostly live in the "shoulds" and "have-tos," adhering to others expectations for you, or from a place of inner truth?

18: Are you aware that you feel unworthy of being free?

19: What is one thing you would change about yourself if you could? Why?

20: What would you do if it was your last day on Earth?

21: How has your family influenced you?

22: Who or what is your biggest trigger and causes the biggest reaction for you?

23: What shame do you hold onto? Where did these feelings originate?

24: Are you always looking in the past or projecting into the future? Is the present moment a part of your day?

25: What are you most terrified of?

26: When presented with something—an invite, an opportunity, etc.—do you say "yes" or "no" as your first response?